DEDICATIONS

I dedicate this book first to my beautiful mother, Deloris Beasley. I'm truly grateful for your belief in me and never abandoning me. If every child had a mother like you this would be a loving world. I further dedicate this book to my sister, Artavia Knight, and my children Shemari Beasley, Davonica Beasley, and Omar Beasley Jr. I love you all, the whole Beasley family!

Last but not least, a special shout out the best Attorney, Caroline Durham. Thank you so much for your assistance. And your dedication to not only myself, but the many others you all help along the way. It's truly a blessing to have met all of you!
I speak on behalf of myself and my family when I say thank you for being there during one of the toughest times of my life, I appreciate you. Thank you.

ACKNOWLEDGEMENTS

First of all, I would like to thank God for allowing me to reveal a talent in me I never knew existed. It's too bad I had to come to prison to find this out! A special thanks to all the readers and supporters of my work. I want to first thank JC at Midwest Bonding, who knew I always had it in me! "Talent" Thank you for believing in me and supporting my projects.

It's truly a blessing to be able to do something that you enjoy doing; while at the same time knowing it brings pleasurable entertainment into the hearts of others.

To all of my aspiring authors, don't let anyone stop your dream. Always have that motivation; drive you had when you were on them blocks. Believe this it's real companies who lost vision on my projects and thanks to them I kept on pushin and came up with BWMP 'Books With a Message Publishing'. And shouts out to the convicts behind bars...We DO have a voice.

Shouts out to my nigga Twenty and King-Knight, and Thirst Ball G. Also Zack, Roy, Young Buck, Young Jeezy, and Young niggas on a come up!

A special shout out to Derrick Johnson, I see you BOY! BWMP Lets get it! Katina its mad love to you and Andy for stepping on board.

Fighting this frame has made me strong and I refuse to be still. I had to do something to get my mind right! Cut the check BWMP!

CHAPTER 1

Delores grew up in Memphis, Tn. She was a southern girl who believed in working hard and maintaining an honest living. It was a sunny afternoon in May, the day a man pulled up alongside her as she was walking down the street. He was driving a cocaine white 2014 Aston Martin, with all white leather seats. Stitched into the headrest of his seats in black, cursive lettering was his name…'*Big Slim*'.

He rolled down the window, and asked Delores, "Whats cookin' good lookin'?"

She replied, "Nothin. Just on my way home from work."

Slim asked, "You wanna go get somethin' to eat, baby?"

"Sure!" she replied, as she hopped into his car and they drove off towards the Waffle House.

Now, before you get all upset and worked up about Delores jumping into a strange man's car, who could very well be the crazed offspring of Ted Bundy. It should be known that Slim and Delores have known each other since grade school and grew up together. At one point, their friendship turned into love and Delores became the mother of his child. Slim was very proud of his son, always calling him "Little T". Slim would take that boy everywhere he went.

Later on, back at their home, Delores argued with Big Slim. They argued a lot, because Slim was a big time dope dealer. Delores was growing tired of it, and wanted him to change his ways.

"You can't be keep bringin' that dope shit around our son!" yelled Delores.

Slim had grown tired of her nagging and trying to control what he does, so he yells back, "This is how I put food on the table for our family!"

Delores fired back, "Had I known at first when we got together so long ago that you were involved in criminal activity, I woulda never even looked twice at your sorry ass!"

"You know what, bitch," Slim retorted. "I grew up poor! My mom and dad never provided me with nothin'. I had to go get it from the mud and grind to come up cuz' no one gave me shit! And that is why to this day, if my son don't grow up to be a smart man and make something of himself, he'll always be plugged to a Mexican cartel!"

Slim had been getting his dope[1]e from Mexico for years.

Delores threw her hands up in frustration and said, "See fool! That's how dumb you is! That's why your ass is gonna end up back in Club Fed!"

---

[1] Ties To The Streets
Ties To The Streets

"Bitch, I don't need you burning bread on me!"

"Well, I don't want our son growin' up without a father!"

The thought softened Slim's tone and agreed, "That, baby doll, I understand."

Slim had to get ready to go out of town. He asked Delores, "Have you seen my passport?"

She replied, "Yeah, baby, it's in the front drawer."

Slim grabbed his wallet out and handed her some cash, and in his best Terminator impression, he turned to her and said "I'll be back." As he headed out the door he called up his lieutenant, Snake, and told him to get ready to go to Mexico.

When Snake and Slim arrived at the airport, they did as always and bought their tickets to Mexico on the spot and paid all cash. This made Snake nervous, because of the seriousness of what they could face if they were to get caught. Normally, Snake was considered a beast in the streets. But when it came to flying down to **Apatizingan Michocan, Mexico** and playing by *'Caballelos Templamos'* cartel rules; he was more of a paranoid scardy cat. But who wouldn't be when you're doing business in a city that is also known as *"The city of death'* because bodies lying around was not out of the ordinary?

Snake turned to Slim and said, "Bro, we cannot keep paying for these tickets with cash money. We be drawin' too much attention to ourselves."

Slim shook his head and replied, "Man, shut your scary ass up!'

"You aint ever gonna listen, man," Snake countered. 'One day, you gonna wish you listen to me, Slim. But don't wait until we sitten in the joint somewhere havin to listen to them cracker jacks tellin us what the fuck to do. Then you'll be sitten there cryin' talkin like 'Man! I wish I woulda listened to my buddy Snake, and then my musty ass wouldn't be here!"

"Man, you need to shut the fuck up! You worse than my baby mama with all that cryin' shit. I shoulda left your punk ass back in Memphis!"

Disappointed, Snake rebuffed, "You know what your problem is? You don't wanna listen to no one with good advice."

"Enough with that bullshit! Grab that luggage and let's roll," Slim ordered.

"Don't be talkin to me like I'm your duboy. Every time we be goin to see them wetbacks, you be actin like your El mother fuckin Chapo himself."

Slim rolled his eyes and asked "Bro, what time our plane pullin up?"

"Nine-fifteen," Snake answered. "Say, should we be hittin up the bar for a few tequila shots?"

"God damn, you gotta be drunk as a skunk every time we be handling our business?" Slim asked. "And you got jokes too? Who you think you is? Bernie Mac?"

"Bernie Mac?! And hell yeah I need some shots!" Snake responded. "I need some liquid courage dealing with your stupid ass! By the way, what we totin' in them bags today?"

Slim replied, "Two-million dollars in cash."

"Man! You is a dumb ass! We about to carry this shit through customs?! And you wonder why I gotta be drunk every time. I swear on everything this is the last trip I take with you to visit these wetbacks. Make El Chapo and his mules come get this shit next time you need help."

Slim wasn't fazed by Snake being so reluctant to assist him. He was confident that he could outsmart anyone including any police if it ever came down to that. And if Snake didn't want to do the job, Slim knew he would have no problem finding someone else to do it. There was a line of cats just waiting to make the kinda cash Slim was paying Snake.

Reminding Snake of this, Slim says, "You know what, Snake? You can be like Eddie Murphy in 'Coming to America" and go to workin at McDonalds, cuz I pay your ass thirty to forty g's a trip just to watch my back. So you shouldnt have too much to say about nothin'."

"Hey Slim, we 'bout to walk through customs, so you better hope that luggage don't set off some alarms through x-ray. These airports aren't the same since them ragheads flew them planes into those towers. You know that beefed up security all over the world. Bro, I might be comin off harsh on you, but I

really need you to make sure your next move is your best move."
Snake was obviously worried about what Slim had planned.

"Bro," Slim responded, "I don't take it like that....For
real man.....that's why I fuck with you. You always see shit
coming. You joke around, but you can always call good
money."

They had made it through customs, going up to gate 15
to Cancun, and got ready to board the plane. As they
approached, Snake spotted two white men at the beginning of the
line staring them down suspiciously. Trying not to tip them off,
Snake whispered to Slim, "By the gate, them two guys look like
alphabet boys."

Slim grimaced, "Man...don't be actin so paranoid!"

As soon as Slim finished saying that, the two men
approached them and the one on the left began speaking first,
"Hello gentlemen! Where are you two headed today?"

Snake quickly snapped back, "Well, sirs, as you can see
by what the gate says we sure as hell aint goin to Siberia."

The same man replied, "Well with that smart remark, we
might just have to go ahead and detain you gentlemen."

Slim interrupted, "Were just goin to Cancun to catch us
a good time."

Finally, the other man spoke, "Well, you gentlemen be
careful down there. Do not go meet with any cartels, because we
will find out and have to prevent you from re-entering the United

States. We're with the DEA. Have a good time in Cancun." He smirked at Slim and Snake, and they walked away.

Slim glanced over at Snake with an irritated look, pissed that he would talk back to them agents knowing what they had going on. But the two men were relieved, knowing that they just dodged a bullet, and boarded their plane to paradise.

They made it to Apatizigan Michoacan safely. Although the town's population is over 100,000 people, most of the streets and buildings are rundown and dusty. The smell of blood in the air in this cold city. Slim and Snake were going to see the Perez brothers at Casa de Perez. They lived in a big house with red Spanish tiles covering the Stucco structure, six bedrooms, 2 ½ showers, and a Jacuzzi. There was a factory that sat behind the house, which is where they produced the heroin. Then behind that, sat another factory where they produced the cocaine. Within the walls of the estate, sat a farm where they grew beans, corn, and the marijuana.

A wrought iron gate and a guardhouse greeted Big Slim and Snake when they arrived. There were a few Mexican soldiers armed with AR-15 assault rifles that approached their vehicle as they pulled into the driveway. Without speaking, the soldiers escorted the two men into the house. As they walked in they were greeted by Jose Perez. He was a short man with a scar above his right eye. He says to Slim in Spanish "Nunez es huca. Confie en hinguno." Translation: *Never trust no one.*

He continued, "Ninguno estuvo en este jueto en 56 anos," *I have been in this game for 56 years.* "Mi amigo jo puedo mandaellh trailer a ta estado lleno de mota dos tomeladas de coca pol." *My friend, I will send an 18-wheel trailer to your state filled with marijuana and two tons of coke.* Continuing in Spanish, Jose then asks "Can you handle this, amigo?"

Slim and Snake both understood and spoke Spanish as well.

Slim replies in Spanish, "All I have in this world is my balls and my word. I don't break that for no one. And just to let you know amigo, I came here with two million dollars in cash."

Pleased to hear this Jose replies, "No problemo. Your grandfather was a great friend of mine. Mi casa es su casa." *My home is your home.*

Speaking in Spanish, Snake chimes in, "Because of the tougher custom laws back in the States, is there a place on our side of the fence where we can make payment arrangements?"

"Buen luga pala dejan dinero," Jose answers. *A good place to drop off the money,* "is Phoenix, Arizona." Jose then hops on the phone to charter a private jet back to Memphis for Slim and Snake, so they didn't have to deal with customs again.

CHAPTER 2

Big Slim and Snake make it back to Memphis safely. On their way back to Slim's from the airport they began to discuss the previous day's events and what could have happened had they not taken that private jet home.

"You know Snake," Slim said as he was driving, "I love you bro. The shit we be doin' seems unreal. So I might come off to you as scary, but the shit we be doin' could land us in the penitentiary for the rest of our lives."

Snake replied, "You know, bro, this shit is not a drill. It's for real, and any given day, the DEA could fall out the fuckin' sky. I ain't ever been to no fed joint, and I know you don't ever wanna go back. You just had your son and everything. That should mean something to ya. So basically, what I'm tellin you is to work smart not hard."

"Lemme tell ya my message, Snake. Sex, money, or murder is the game we play. Jail or death is what they say. Chances make champions. Which side you gon' take?"

Snake thinks for a second, then replies "That's some serious shit yer talkin'. But man, you's a stupid motherfucker goin through customs like that! I do take chances, Slim, but they are calculated. What we did through customs is damn near crazy and coulda popped us off!"

"Well hopefully we don't have to see the penitentiary, but if we do, I'm gonna take mine like a man," says Slim.

Sensing that Slim was implying that he was a snitch, Snake replies, "So what the fuck is you sayin', bro? Trying to call me Donnie Brosko or something?

"No bro, I'm not calling you no snitch. I'm just trying to tell you if something were to happen, I'd be takin it like a man," explains Slim.

"You ain't got no other fuckin' choice," Snake retorts, "cuz El Chapo of the Perez brothers be comin' up here and choppin' your tongue off!" And they both started cracking up.

"Boy Snake," Slim says after catching his breath from laughing so hard. "I love hangin' out with you. You funny as hell, bro!"

Changing the conversation to a more serious subject, Snake asks Slim, "What was it like in the joint, bro?"

"When I was first housed in the joint, I was in Beckley, Virginia. That was a medium-high security federal prison. You'd have motherfucka's stealing bell peppers and onions from the kitchen. Gambling to make a living and survive." Slim reminisced, "Me on the other hand, I grabbed a degree in paralegal. And that's how I came off a thirty-year sentence."

Surprised that his friend had a degree, Snake replies, "Damn, you a smart motherfucker, bro. But it seems to me that the smarter ya get, your stupid ass gets dumber too. You right back out here floodin' the streets with this dope, and movin fast as a motherfucker. You gone from zero to one hundred real quick. You've only been out six months, and you've accumulated more than one of them tight ends from the Tennessee Titans."

Slim said, "Bro, ain't no sense of me lying to myself about change. I knew what I was gonna do from day one when they let me out of R.D.," the release department in federal prison. "Guess who was up there with me? Funny ass SJ. He just came home back to Detroit. And my other partner, JB, just got out, and he up in Minnesota. He just got out of Sandstone. These are the dudes that I'm gonna give these bricks to."

Snake frowned, "Them nigga's just as stupid as you! They ain't been out for thirty days, and they already up to their ass in El Chapo shit, not wanting to give themselves a chance. Lemme ask ya somethin', Slim. How your motherfuckin' P.O. feel about this? You drivin around in a brand new 2014 Bentley truck, and you got all this shit sittin' on Forges rims. Big dummy, you know what you sayin' when you do stupid shit like this? You got a big neon sign flashin' over ya head. You on some high power shit like the B.M.F.!

"This fool, Big Meech, had big billboard signs sitting right off the highways in Atlanta sayin' 'The world is ours!' He had a network worth 227 million dollars. Are you trying to go that route? Cuz' if you is, please leave Snake outta that shit."

"Bro," Slim replied, "the route already been started. You know how many bricks we gonna get? You be always doin' stupid shit, too! I signed ya up for a lifetime bid! Let's get to it! I'm gonna front you 200 kilos."

Snake says, "Aww hell no! Boss, ya better rethink that crap! You gonna have El Chapo after MY ass! Put that shit on one of your other duboys."

"Bro, bro, all bullshit aside, I'm gonna front Corey some work and let him hold down south Memphis. Then, I'm gonna hit up my homie Bubba-Lee, and front him some bricks so he can light up north Memphis. Then, I'm gonna send some shit up to my boy JB in Minnesota. I'm actually thinkin' about movin' there. It's a real nice state, and they gots that big ass mall up there called "Mall of America." My only competition there would be the Hoodrich Boys. Now, there's this nigga that I use to guck with named Big O. He fell out of Minnesota and caught a fed case. Big O was gettin money mothfucka, man! Probably gonna go up there and get it in with my niggas JB and O." Slim continued, "Matter of fact, I talked to O last week and he got some soldiers up there from Block-Money and he told me this is how he gonna run the organization; He said he gonna front B 300 birds. Then he gonna use Thirst-Ball for security when Big

O and I move through the town, cuz Thirst-Ball is a killer from the Gardens Projects in Chicago. And B will feed Reese money. O is also so wrapped up in his rap career, he gots a few artists. One of them is named King Knight. O done dropped about 2 million dollars on Knight. But knight just wanna dib and dab in the game when O be tryin to tell him to keep followin his career. Knight still a shooter, though. Sounds to me like O got that area in a choke hold. He just needs product moved in. What you think about that?"

Snake pauses and thinks about everything Slim just told him, then answers, "Seems to me you be fallin' under the Rico Act. Continuin' criminal enterprises as if a U.S. Attorney was to get you, he would roast your ass like a cornish hen!"

Shakin his head, Slim replies, "I ain't worried 'bout that U.S. Attorney crap! I'm gonna keep some money, so that if I was ever to fall, I'd have a lawyer to buy the case."

"Boy," Snake snickered, "you ain't learned shit! Don't you know the feds print the money!"

Just then, Slim's phone rang.

"Hello," Slim answers the phone.

"Hello my fuckin' ass," Delores says on the other end. "How long you been back in town? Don't' you know you have a fuckin' family? All you wanna do is sell dope day and night. Whatever happened to spendin' quality time with me and your son? Seems to me your drugs are your main priority. Little T is growin up without his dad. You is missin' the best parts of his life, Slim. He growin' up to be a man at 14 years old. I went to his football game. What am I supposed to tell him? His daddy at work? Providing us with, and I stress this, an honest livin? Or he's a forecaster, makin' it snows with white coke?"

"Bitch," Slim retorts, "you best be stayin off my phone talkin' like that. And Delores, stop makin' me lose focus out here while I be makin' moves out here in the street. I make one bad move, and this whole operation is dead."

Delores cuts in, "That's all you think about, right? Makin' moves. So you know what, Slim? I'm thinking about packin' my shit up, and movin' to Minnesota. Ya know what? I gotta take my son away from this illegal shit."

"Delores, open the garage for me. I'm pullin' in now."

"That still don't change nothin," Delores says. Then she shouts out away from the phone, "Little T!! Open the garage for our daddy!"

Little T opens the garage door, and Slim pulls in. Slim and Snake hop out of the car, and Little T says, "Hey dad! What's up?"

"Nothin, lil pimpin," Slim answers. "What's happenin' with you? How's school?"

"It was okay, dad," Little T answers. "I wanted you to be at my football game, but you wasn't there. But I still won, dad! 27 to 14."

"That's my junior. Here's $500 for ya."

CHAPTER 3

.

       The next day, Slim wakes his son up for school. They both showered and got dressed. Little T
puts on some True Religion jeans, and a matching shirt, all black. Little T then came to the
kitchen where his dad was.

      "Dad", he asks. "Can I use some of your cologne?"

      "Sure," answered Slim. "Which one you gonna put on?"

      "Daddy, you know I gotta use that Gene Paul. It smells just like you."

      "Son, you becomin' a fly motherfucka, like your dad."

      "Dad, you now I'm a stunner."

      "Son, I see you got them waves for the babes."

      "Yeah, dad. I got my three-sixty goin'. Say, could I wear your chains, pretty please?"

"Little T, you wanna wear a thirty-thousand-dollar chain to school?"

"Pretty please, pops?" Pleads Little T.

"Go ahead, but hurry up son. I gotta get you to school. It's starting to get late and I don't wanna hear your mama's mouth."

"Dad," Little T continues. "Can you please bring me in the Benz?"

Slim said, "Boy, bring your ass on."

They get in the Benz S 550, all black. Slim cuts on the stereo, and pulls out of the garage. T tells his dad, "cut Big O on." The music was thumping and coming out real clear. T was rapping along to Big O's lyrics. ***"Keep it real with the niggas that keep it real with me. I play the game the way it supposed to be."*** As they were driving along, a car pulls up behind them, about one car length back. Little T spots it in the mirror, but thinks nothing of it.

"Dad, I love how Big O be spittin' that real shit."

"Boy," his dad scolding him, "stop all that cussin'!"

"Dad, why ain't Mac-E not signed to Big O.E.N.T. no more?"

As they pulled around the corner, the car behind them also pulled around the corner. Little T keeps an eye on the car.

Slim replied, "it was on Hip Hop Worldstar that Mac-E was out in Detroit, and the manager, Zinc, said on national T.V.

that Mac-E did some cutthroat shit. He went and fucked one of O's native chicks' while they was recording a song in Michigan. Lemme tell you somethin', son! Never fuck your man's chick. That's probably why your man Yo gotti never signed Mac-E. O was just trying to provide a decent living for Mac-E. O always had love for this guy, and will continue to do so. But, it just ain't the same between them no more 'cuz Mac-E broke their friendship from the move he put down. Back in Big O's old days, this coulda started some major beefs in the music industry, but O left the shit alone, tryin' to be the better man. He raised Mac-E, and it hurt him bad that Mac-E would pull some hoe shit like that. Just to sum it up, how'd you think I'd feel if Snake did that to your mom?"

"Well, dad, with me being your son, I already know how you'd feel. I'd body his ass if he pulled something like that with mom," answered Little T.

"Son, it seems you be growin' to be a lil' gangster."

"Dad, if somethin' was to ever happen to you; you ain't gotta worry about how me and mom are gonna make it. Because, I'm cut from the same cloth you're cut from, and that's gangsta for life. I love ya, pops."

Little T sees some movement from the car behind them. They turn a corner,] and the car behind them also turns the corner. T then catches movement from the passenger side.

"Dad," says Little T with concern, "I'm noticin' two white boys in a Ford Taurus followin' us. I didn't wanna seem paranoid, but he looks like he's snapping a picture of ya."

"Alright son," Slim sounding cautious, "we pullin' up to your school. I need you to pay attention."

Slim removed his phone from his belt. "Here's my phone. Text your mother while she's at work, and let her know not to go back to the house. Have her come get you after school, and to go get a hotel room. I'm gonna get someone to pack the house up so we can move to Minnesota. I think the Feds are watching me."

Little T takes the phone and starts typing the message to his mother. Slim turns into the school's driveway. The car behind them slows down and pulls to the side of the road. Slim pulls up to the drop-off zone, and stops. He reaches into the center console of his car and pulls out a wad of cash.

"Here's five grand. Put it in your book bag," and Slim hands the wad of cash to Little T. "Don't worry son, everythin' will be alright." Little T finishes the text, and hands the phone back to his dad, and takes the cash, and puts it in his bag.

"Daddy, I'll never sweat. Just don't let them people knock you off," he tells Slim.

"I love you son. Now go on into school."

Little T got out of the car and walked toward the doors of his school. He observed the car following his dad as Slim pulled out of the driveway. Little T thinks to himself, *'If they take my daddy down, they'd done nothin' but slow us down. I'd need to step up and pick up where he left off.'*

CHAPTER 4

Slim was pushing through traffic when he noticed another car following him. As he was approaching a stop light. He held his right hand up, flips the finger and accelerates through a yellow light. The cars following him never had a chance and were forced to stop at the light as it changed to red. Slim turned onto Jackson Street. When he saw no more cars were following him, he pulled onto Randie Street, he saw one of his soldiers outside of their house. Slim pulls up alongside of him, rolls his window down and says,

"Hey Corey, what's up partner?"

"Not much, man," Corey said, outside in his yard. "Pull up in the back of the house because Vice has been very hot in the neighborhood. Agents been sitting in unmarked cars all through this bitch. They've been rollin' like a motherfucka."

Slim whipped around to the back, parked his car, and got out. Corey was right there to greet him.

"Man, I'm glad you pulled up. I got a quarter million in cash in the attic. I'm about to run in and get it for ya." Slim says as he notices another squad car zoom past the house as Corey was inside. When Corey was coming back, Slim lets Corey in on what's going on. "You know what, Corey? It's hot as a motherfucka out here. You best be cleaning up for the rest of the day. You don't want them Jakes to run into your crib. We were lucky that 18 wheeler made it through customs, but the heat's coming' down, man."

Corey nods, and Slim continues, "Lemme give ya some advice, bro. You have a natural talent for your work, and over time you'll become quite the expert I picked you to be. You'll command a high fee for what you do, which will help several people at once."

Corey replies, "you, yourself, have something fresh to add to the mix, bro, and shouldn't hesitate for a moment to add it. Slim, be confident! The world needs your input. Vitality will sweep over you the moment you put your two cents in."

Slim and Corey always get philosophical with each other when the pressure was on.

Slim says, "Just because you live your life, doesn't mean you know it. You'll learn your reasons
from previously misunderstood events."

"What makes you say that Slim?" Corey asks.

"Just look around you Corey. Signs and symbols are for the conscious mind. Before a storm,
comes a warning. I hope you cleaned up in here. I'm on my way to keep picking up this cash."

"Alright, Slim. Work smart and not hard."

"I'm gone, bro," Slim says and they shook hands and bro-hugged each other.

Slim tossed the bag of money in the trunk, closed it, and got back into his car. He jumped on
highway 240 west, heading toward Germantown where Snake lived. He came up off the exit, pulled off the street, picked up his phone, and called Snake.

"What's up boy? Where you at?"

"Man," Snake answered, "don't be asking me where I'm at, callin' me this fuckin' early in the
morning at ten-fifteen. I'm at home." Click. Snake hung up.

Just as he was hanging up, Slim was ringing his doorbell. Snake answers the door,

"I guess you don't get the message that I don't wanna be bothered this early in the mornin' when I hung up on your ass!"

"You're my brother, man. I can come wake your ass up wheneva I want. And by the way,
you should be glad that I'm waking you up."

Snake scolded Slim, "You better have a good damn reason waking me up this early with all
these white folks around. Hell, I never get up this early! I stay in a gated community where we don't run in and out! So, know that you ain't leaving my house real quick."

Slim enters the house and says, "Hey, bro, you're the one who put me on the 'allowed entrance' list!" Slim uses finger quotes when he states it.

"True that, but I wasn't expecting you to wake my ass up! Now why'd you come over this
Early?"

"Well," Slim answers, "I've got some good news and some bad news. Which one you want first?"

"Spit it out motherfucka. I ain't got time for this good news bad news shit!" Snake remarked.

"Well, bro," Slim states, "the Feds have been following me around and..."

"WHAT THE FUCK YOU SAY?" Snake interrupted and hollered. "Get your hot ass out my house! I ain't having this El Chapo shit brought down on me. By the way, I got one point two million dollars I ran through the counter three times, so you don't need to count it."

Snake runs upstairs, and comes back down a few seconds later with two duffel bags.

Get this crap outta my house before I get slapped down."

"Bro," Slim says, "I'm movin' up to Minnesota. Shits been gettin' to hot here in Memphis. And also, I already talked to my real estate agent. She found a house in Prior Lake, MN, near an Indian Casino. This house, Snake, is a bad motherfucka. It costs seven hundred and ninety-eight thousand dollars."

"See," Snake interrupts again. "You's a dumb motherfucka! Why don't you just call the U.S. Attorney and tell them, 'hey I sell dope!' I'm a regular El Chapo. Please make my bed up at the pen and lock my dumb ass up! Seems like you ain't gonna be enjoying that shit too long, Slim. You don't even have an income to justify that! Go on, tell me the square footage of the place. Go on, tell me motherfucka."

Slim answers, "Ten-thousand. It has a three car garage, six bedrooms, two Jacuzzis, a game room, an elevator, a basketball courts, swimming pool, a tennis court, and a finished basement."

Snake starts shakin' his head, "It seems like to me you've taken yourself out of the little league, and moved straight to the majors. You be messin' up everyone's lives. I'm not tryin' to go eat dinner with Bernie Maddoff, and I know where he at. He's in North Carolina in a fed house called Butler. That's a medium security joint. See, you know what it is Slim? It's like every time you go to the barbershop, you pick out lots of barbers, and it seems like none of them can cut to you, but sooner or later, you gonna meet the right barber, and you gonna get a fade! Who gonna be doin' the fadin', Snake?"

Snake answers, "Either the western district of Tennessee or the U.S. District of Minnesota."

Slim replies, "That's what you be doin' when the heats on. You be burning my bread."

Snake says, "Why you say that? You smart, but you don't be usin' your head when it really matters."

Slim replies, "Man don't become successful without failure. He becomes successful because he don't let failure stop him."

Snake replies, "You always got somethin' real smooth to say when you don't want to deal with the truth, but lemme tell ya, Slim. The truth don't need no support, remember this, and I ain't tryin' to be funny. No one, not even the actors who played James Bond is actually James Bond. You keep on thinkin' we can't be touched. We can, because you be movin' reckless, buyin' all them expensive cars, houses, jewelry, and shit."

Slim replies, "Maybe you're watchin' to see what happens, and that is not the same, never the
same as just waiting around. Observation is the art of confident people."

Snake sarcastically says, "Okay, Socrates."

"Hold on Snake, lemme call Two Men and a Truck, and have them move my stuff out."
Slim calls them up.

"Hello," a woman answers, "Two Men and a Truck. How can I help you today?"

Slim responds, "Yes, I was wondering if I could get an estimate on moving my furniture and cars
to Prior Lake, Minnesota from Memphis?"

"Hold on please, sir." She accesses her computer and types in the source and destination
cities, and then asks, "What day would you need it moved?"

"As soon as possible."

"Okay, one moment, please." She types a few more strokes on the keyboard and replies, "as
early as six-fifteen tomorrow morning."

Slim replied, "Good."

The woman says, "That would be nine thousand, six hundred and eighty-nine dollars, and forty-five cents. How would you be paying for this?"

Slim answers, "Cashier's check, if you accept that."

She responds back, "Sure we can, sir. When do you plan on dropping that off?"

"I can probably have that to you as early as five this afternoon."

"That will be perfect. We close at six this evening. Thank you for choosing us for our moving needs. Can I have your name, your current address and the address of your new home, please?"

Slim gave her the relevant information, thanked her, and hung up.

"Damn," Snake said afterward. "You really is leavin' me."

"Yeah, bro," Slim replies. "Shit's gettin' really tight here. I already have Delores holed up at a hotel." Slim's phone then rings. He answers. "You have a collect call from Corey Walker. If you wish to accept this call, press five. To refuse this call, press nine…"

Snake overheard this and shouts out, "PRESS NINE MAN, PRESS NINE! Feds be listenin' in!"

"Man," Slim tried to calm Snake down. "I can't be doin' that Corey's my boy."

Slim pressed 5. After hearing the charges, the recorded voice then said, "This call shall be recorded and subject to monitoring at any time."

"Hang it up Slim, I'm tellin' ya." Snake pleads again.

"Hello," Slim says into the phone.

Corey says, "th…. they found the hundred birds…."

"WHAT!" Slim shouts.

"They found two forty-five pistols," Corey continues, but Slim hears his voice crackling.

"Don't worry man," Slim tries to calm Corey down. "If you get a burn, I'll get you out."

Corey, crying into the phone, says, "Slim, I'm trying to keep a cool booty!"

Immediately Slim hangs up.

Snake jumps up, "Slim, I told ya they gonna pop you sooner or later. The boy gonna tell! So grab your meals and let your wheels goes elsewhere to do deals, 'cuz the Feds are out to kill!"

"I'm outta here dawg. We'll talk later," Slim says. He then walks to his car, gets in, and drives up to the bank to get his cashier's check ready for the moving company.

CHAPTER 5

      While Slim finished making arrangements for the move the next day, Corey sat in a white
washed walled cell with paint chipping off, and graffiti from Slim back when he caught his fed
case. It read: I hate rats. It was like Slim was haunting Corey down right there in the cell. Two federal agents were sitting in the other room, giving each other high fives. One spoke to two Shelby County deputies and told them, "Bring Corey Walker to room five."

The deputies went to Corey's cell, and one asked him, "would you like to speak with federal agents?"

"Y-y-yes sir." Corey said, timidly.

"C'mon then, man," the other one said, and they escorted him to interview room five where the two agents were waiting. The deputies shackled Corey to a chair. Agents Brown and Walker sat across from Corey.

Agent Brown says, "Let me read you your Miranda rights before we go any further. You have the right not to speak with us. If you should choose to speak, anything you say to us can and could possibly be used against you. You can have an attorney present while we question you, or you may consult with one before We do so. If you can't afford one, one will be provided to you by the public defender's office. But Agent Walker and I believe that you would like to get out of here quickly, don't you Corey? It seems like to me, Corey, that you were moving a little too fast. Before we go any further, do you understand the rights we said to you?"

Corey, again timidly, says. "Y-y-yes, sir."

Agent Brown continued, "Would you like to help yourself out, Corey?"

Corey responds, "Help myself, how?"

Brown replies, "You're looking at a lifetime sentence in the federal system for all those illegal substances we found in your house. Not only that, you qualify as a career offender."

Corey says, "You don't need to do no more talkin'. What do you need to know?"

"We want to talk about Big Slim and his buddy Snake," Brown says.

"Well," Corey fidgeting as he speaks, "To be honest, I don't know nothin' 'bout Snake, but there is plenty I can tell ya about Big Slim."

Brown asked, "how much cocaine does Slim give you?"

Corey answers, "Five hundred keys every month."

"Do you think, if we let you go, you could do a controlled buy from Big Slim?"

"Yes," Corey answers again, "But it would look a little fishy 'cuz I just called him and because you guys just popped me."

Brown replies, "We're aware of that. We just want you to act normal. We would monitor you from the phone we're giving you," and Brown pulls out a cell phone.

"Yeah," Corey says.

"Okay," Brown says and hands the phone to Corey. "Call him again, but wait a sec while I plug in this device to record the call." Brown plugs in a digital recorder to the phone.

"Alright we're all set. Place the call." Corey punches in Slim's cell number, his fingers shaking

with each push of a digit. The phone rings. On the fourth ring,
Slim picks up,

"What's up? Who's this?"

Corey responds, "it's me, bro."

"Bro? Who? Corey? Get the fuck out! You working
with them people?"

Corey answers, "hell no! I ain't playing games with you,
bro. W-where can I meet you at tomorrow? I need a buy."

Slim says, "What? I can't hear you. My phone's
fuckin' up."

Click. Slim hangs up.

Agent Brown says, "You did a good job, Corey. You
just tied his ass into a conspiracy. And
tomorrow, you call us by eleven-thirty a.m." Agent Brown turns
to the door and shouts, "Deputy! You can take him back to be
released."

One of the deputies says, "Damn, boy! You told them
the whole truth and nothin' but the truth,
and you get released like that?" And the deputies unshackle him
from the chair and escort him out to booking to be released.

When Slim got the call from Corey, he was already on
94 west in the Escalade, coming out of Rockford, Illinois paying
a toll, just about to pass the sign "Welcome to Wisconsin".
Delores and Little T were with him.

Delores asks, "Who was that? Corey? You best be stayin' off the phone with him. When you said we were movin' to Minnesota, you were gonna leave all that garbage behind."

"You're right about that," Slim responds. "I'm just so makin' sure this shits clear.

Anybody have to use the bathroom?"

"Yeah, daddy, I gotta drain the weasel of mine," Little T says.

"Boy, watch that language with your mama in the car!" Delores says.

They take exit 232 into the Flyin' J truck shop. They all hop out of the Escalade after Slim pulls up to pump fifteen. Little T and Delores run in to use the bathroom. Slim pulls out his cell phone and calls Snake.

"Hello, Snake answers. "Me speak no English."

"C'mon, Snake, I know it's you."

"No Snake, no longer this number. What, man? I told you not to call this number no more."

"Guess what, bro? Corey's out."

Snake replies, "Where I'm from, we call that *'Cuapo'*. People like that gotta move their family to Briaco. 'Cuz I'm puttin' in one call, and that's to El Chapo."

Click Snake hangs up.

"Man," Slim says to himself, "I'm gonna miss that boy, he crazy as hell." He walks into

Flyin' J, goes to the counter person, and says, "Gimme fifty-five on pump fifteen."

Delores approaches, "Gimme a fifty-dollar monopoly scratch off, and two of those Lucky seven's. I'm gonna scratch them off right here at the counter because I like to scratch them in the store and know if I'm a winner or not."

Little T then walks up and asks, "Can I get a burger, a soda, and some chips, dad?"

"Sure," Slim answers. "Get your dad a Mt. Dew and mom a Dr. Pepper."

After Slim pays for the gas, food, and scratch offs, Delores takes the tickets, and scratches them off, starting with the Lucky Sevens. She won $19,000. Then she does the Monopoly ticket, and wins $150,000. Delores and Little T start jumping up and down, hooting and hollering. The cashier immediately says,

"Congratulations, but you're gonna have to mail those in. It's too big for us to cash here."

They all walk back to the Escalade, Slim pumps the gas, sayin' "Ooo wee, it's chilly as a motherfuck here. Hey baby, grab one of them dutches outta the glove box and some of that Nigerian Nightmare. Could you roll that up for me, baby doll?" Delores rolls up a blunt. Slim finishes pumping the gas, hops back into the truck, and drives back onto the highway. Slim smoking his stogie was doing one-hundred miles per hour, bumpin' Rick Ross, heading to Minnesota. He's going so fast he hit Eau Claire, WI in no time.

Delores says, "Boy, you better be slowin' down. These state troopers don't fuck around." Just as she was saying that, they were passing through Hudson. A State Trooper caught up behind him, flashing his lights.

"Son," Slim says to Little T, "grab that chronic killer and spray the truck down so it don't smell like weed in here. I don't know if he's gonna pull us over, but he's riding my ass." The State Trooper shoots past them and pulls over a truck in front of them. They make it to Minnesota, when Slim's phone rings.

"Hello?" Slim answers, "This Corey. I know who this is."

"Meet me at the B.B. King restaurant on Bills Street. One hour."

"Okay, bro," and Slim hangs up. After another 45 mins, Slim pulls into their driveway of their new home.

Little T says, "Ooo, dad, this is nice."

Delores kisses him and says, "This is a home. Now you can keep your ass off of workin' the streets."

They all walk into the house and they all go to their bedrooms, because they were exhausted from their trip.

Back in Memphis, Agents were setting up their surveillance teams. As they planned at the previous days meeting, they gave Corey their marked money to make the controlled buy purchase. Then set up an audio and video recording device hidden on his jacket. After two hours had passed, Big Slim was a no show. Every time Corey tried to call Slim's phone, a message saying, 'The subscriber has travelled outside of the coverage area. Please try your call again later.' Slim was long gone.... eluding the DEA once again....

CHAPTER 6

Some time had passed since Slim's move from 0-Memphis. Slim, Delores and Little T have been settled in their new home for quite some time now... Little T was sixteen now. One morning in October, Slim shouts down to Little T in the basement,

"Little T, what you doin' down there?"

"Dad," T answers. "Don't call me 'Little T' anymore, call me 'Big T'."

Slim walks down the stairs, and sees Big T dripping with sweat from the master workout.

He asks, "Son, what are ya doin'?"

"Well, pops, I just got done doin' five-hundred burpees, bench pressing 350lbs at fifteen reps of ten, and twenty sets of ten pull-ups. And I even ran on the treadmill for an hour and thirty minutes 'cuz I gotta have my cardio, being a big shot quarterback ya know," Little T said with a cocky tone while flexing his arms for his Dad.

"Damn! T, take that shirt off so I can see that lil' chest of yours."

T, pulling at his shirt, stepping around, says in a tough voice, "Do you want me to do that? Do you really wanna see what's under this hood, pops?"

Slim replied, "Make it understood, son."

T ripped his shirt off, showing nothing but six-pack abs, and muscles that would put Dwayne 'The Rock' Johnson to shame.

Slim shouts, "Damn, son, you rock the fuck up! That looks like a fifty-two sized chest!"

Delores hears the commotion and walks down the stairs. She sees T and starts dancing around and fanning herself, saying, "That's my boy!"

"So, son," Slim says, "You've been up since four-thirty this mornin'. We heard ya down
here."

"Pops, I have to do that. I'm captain of the Prior Lake Lakers football team."

"Son, I know you wanna drive the truck to school today, but I'm gonna follow behind you.
I want to meet your coach, Mr. George."

"That's cool, pops. Lemme shower real quick so I don't be late for school." T then starts
to the bathroom and showers.

After Slim and Delores got dressed, they see Little T, Big T now, making an organic
lemon drink, as well as wheat grass quinoa and kale, with lentils.

"Dad, I inspired my whole team to drink this 'cuz it conditions the body when we're in
games and get hit hard. The bones won't be healing right otherwise." T then asks, "So are you guys gonna be at my homecoming game tonight?"

Delores says, "I had to work today, but I swapped shifts with someone, so I'll be there. The question is will your dad be attending?"

"Man," T replies, "Since we moved from Memphis, dad has been very supportive of me."

Slim says, "Damn straight, I'll be there. I gotta see the beast in action."

They all go into the garage. Slim and Delores climb into the Mercedes. Big T hops into the Escalade. Slim follows the Escalade out, they exit their neighborhood onto County Road 83. They get to County RD. 21 and turn left. At County Road 42, they turn right. After a few miles, they get to County RD. 16, and turn right again. A big wheatgrass field separates the parking lot of Prior Lake High School from the main road. They pull into a long winding driveway. A brick building greets them with a curved glass & white curved architectural structure juts out from the main brown bricked building. Big T parks in the student section. Slim finds a visitor slot close to the main entrance and parks there. Slim and Delores get out and meet their son under the overhang in front of the entrance.

First person they meet inside the school is Mr. Stuart, the principal. He shakes their hand, and tells them, "You have a very nice son and his grades are very outstanding. His football career is outspoken. He's on his way to become the next Michael Vick. He's a great quarterback and inspiration for the school, that's why he's captain of the team."

Mr. Stuart sees Mr. George walk by. "Mr. George. Hey, Mr. George. Come over and meet Tyrell's parents'." T stood for Tyrell.

Mr. George came over and greeted Slim, Delores, and Big T, shaking their hands.

Mr. George says, "My pleasure meeting you, finally."

Slim says, "I'm Cedric Carter," and he gestures towards Delores, "and this is my wife, Delores Carter."

Delores nods and says, "Pleased to meet you."

"I have so many remarkable things to say about your son," continued Mr. George. "But

first, I want to say your son has a unique style out of anyone I have ever seen in my thirteen years of coaching. Already, there are scouts calling from universities wanting him to commit to their school. Cedric, he is so good at what he does, he makes the team believe that they can win every game."

Slim replies, "Well, thank you very much, Mr. George. We all feel very flattered by your praises."

"He is deserving of it, Cedric. And please, call me Coach." Mr. George replies.

Later that night, Prior Lake was 5 and 0 going into their homecoming game against Northfield. Big T was ready for the challenge. As the public address announcer was listing off the starting players to the crowd, he announces Big T next.

"And starting at quarterback is number four, your very own Tyrell Carter!"

The crowd went berserk, chanting "*MVP, MVP, MVP, MVP!*" Big T looked up to the stands, seeing his mom and dad going crazy. He prayed, "God, give me the courage to crush my opponents!"

The referee, Big T, and the visiting team's Captain meet at the center of the Bennet Field to do the coin toss to begin the game.

Its Northfields choice, when the ref turns to their team captain and asks,

"Heads or tails?"

The Captain calls out, "Tails."

But the toss came up heads. The crowd went wild again chanting, *"MVP, MVP, MVP!"*

"We elect to receive," Big T said.

So the players all lined up for the kickoff. Northfield starts the game by kicking the ball off to 'Mathews' receiver of special teams. He catches the ball deep in the end zone, and starts to run down field. But before he could really get moving down the field, three Northfield players were already there, drilling Mathews hard to the ground at the one-yard line. As the players unpile off of Mathews, he was still lying on the ground. He was clutching his foot and crying in agonizing pain.

"Oh my god," Delores starts to worry. "I hope they don't kill my son like that. They are so much bigger than him."

"Shit," Slim says. "That boy is pumpin' three hundred and fifty pounds. You outta see him pump them weights. My boy is gonna score right now. You just watch."

"Not on my son," says a parent of one of the opposing players. "He plays defensive
tackle. My Michael is gonna sack his ass. By the way, did you bring any spare change? Because we can make a side bet."

Slim replies, "Make it lite on yourself."

The parent, Mr. Thomas, scoffs, saying "Buddy, I haul kegs for Anheuser Busch and
make good money. I got ten crispies in my billfold says my Michael pounds your son before he even steps out of the pocket."

"Well," Slim responds, "I'm gonna be generous and put my two-grand to your one
thousand, pal."

Mr. Thomas' face turns cherry red and he says, "You're on, buddy."

The trainers haul Matthews off of the field, with what appears to be a broken foot while the players line up for the next play at the line of scrimmage. Northfield was set up in a nickel defense,
showing blitz. Coach George had Big T lined up in a shotgun formation. Big T calls out the count,

"Forty-nine, forty-eight, hut!"

The center snaps the ball to Big T. Big T pump fakes, comes out of the pocket, and stiff arms Michael Thomas, shoving his ass to the ground. Big T ran for 99 yards for a touchdown.

The crowd goes nuts, again chanting, *"MVP, MVP, MVP!"*

Big T's teammates swarm him in the end zone, high-fiving, and back slapping him. Mr. Thomas, with his jaw dropped in shock and horror, goes into his wallet, and hands Slim the thousand dollars. But then, shaking his awe off, turns to Slim and says,

"Your son got lucky! My son got held. Damn refs need glasses! Wanna bet on the whole game, Mr. Rich man? I got three grand that says Northfield whoops your ass, ya Vegas bookie."

Slim replies, "I got seven grand to your three, that your boy gets shut out."

Mr. Thomas responds, "You got yourself a bet, pal."

After Prior Lake kicks off to Northfield, Northfield took four plays to make it only to their own thirty-five-yard line. On the next play, they fumble and Prior Lake recovers.

"Sonofabitch!" Mr. Thomas shouts, whipping his trucker hat off and throwing it to the ground.

On the very next play, Big T throws a bonk to one of his wide receivers, who caught it right in the end zone, making it a thirty-five-yard touchdown.

Mr. Thomas screaming, "Who the fuck is this kid? Is he even eligible to play?"

The crowd shouts….

"Na-na-na-naaa, na-na-na-naaa. Hey, hey, hey, goodbye!" As the band plays along.

By halftime, Big T ran for one hundred fifty total yards, and threw three more touchdowns. The score read 28 to nothing. By the fourth quarter, he threw another two touchdowns, totaling two-hundred and fifty yards. He rushed for another sixty yards. When the game was over, the final score was forty-two to nothing. Mr. Thomas gave Slim the three grand and said,

"You have a very talented son. I'm going to keep an eye on his career. I know he's going to the NFL."

Slim replied, "Thank you, sir."

After the exchange, a scout walked over and introduced himself,

"My name is Travis Trevino. I'm a scout for the University of Minnesota, the Golden Gophers Football program. I'd like to discuss with you the possibility of a football scholarship sometime."

Delores says, "We would love to talk about that someday, but not right now."

"That's fine, ma'am. Here's my card. We'll talk soon," and the man handed her his card.

As the team walked off the field, they hoisted Big T on their shoulders, and carried him to the locker room. Slim and Delores looked on, proud that the little man they once knew had become a big man...a leader that his school looked up to. Who knows if he would have had this opportunity in Memphis. Slim realized how thankful he was that he moved his family when he did, and changed his ways before it was too late.

CHAPTER 7

Slim was loving the Minnesota atmosphere. Things were starting to look up for him. He wasn't being chased by the authorities. He and Delores were back on good terms, however, she was still keeping a close eye on Slim. She didn't want him indulging in criminal activity again. Despite Delores's prying, Slim felt confident enough to call up his buddie's Big O and JB to talk about possibly hustling again. He calls JB first,

"Where you at, P?" Slim asked when JB answered.

"I'm down at Chicago and Lake St., dawg. What you up to?" JB replies.

"We need to meet up," Slim says. "How about lunch at Benihanas at noon?"

"Sounds like a plan. See ya there, boy." JB replies, and hangs up.

Next, Slim calls Big O. The phone rings.

Big O answers, "Yo dime, my time."

Slim replies, "What up, boy?"

"Who's this? That ain't my boy Slim, is it?"

"Ya, it's your boy Slim. Meet me at Benihanas at noon for some grub. JB gonna be there."

"You fuckin' with old jive ass JB? Listen, man. You don't ever need to mess with him at all.

"I need help with that stuff, bro." Slim replies.

"I'm gonna keep you protected so that nigga's like you don't be exposed. I got a fuckin' A-team here to move all them units. So we don't need to put our hands on it."

Slim replied, "Holdup, man. I don't wanna do too much talking on the phone. We'll discuss business at Beni's."

Big O replies, "I understand, player. I'll holler at you then, bro," and Big O hung up.

Slim jumped in the shower. After drying himself off and spicing himself up, he threw on
his True Religion jumpsuit, all-black Gucci sneakers, sunglasses, diamond-studded platinum crosses, and a presidential gold masterpiece Rolex. He then hopped into his S-550, and took US highway 169 north, to I-394 east to Minnesota State Highway 100 north to Brooklyn Center. He swung by a storage unit to pick up two duffel bags full of cocaine and heroin, 175 keys each. When he jumped back to his car, carrying the bags, a white man approached Slim, scaring him half to death.

The man asked, "Do you need any help with them bags, sir?"

Slim answered, "N-n-no, sir. I-I'm good. Thank you f-f-for the offer." Slim, thinking to himself 'damn, I gotta hurry up and start movin' this shit around.'

Slim bounced back on 100 south to I-394 west and exits onto Louisiana Avenue to get to Benihanas. As Slim parks, he spots Big O pulling up in an all-black 2015 Hellcat Dodge Charger. O slides into a space next to Slim. JB pulls up in a cranberry mahogany Porsche truck right after O parks, and glides into the other space next to Slim. When they all stepped out of their vehicles, bling-bling could not describe the scene. JB had on about 80 grand worth of jewelry. Big O had on his buff Cartier glasses, and a Franck Muller watch worth about 90 thousand, and additional jewelry worth an estimated 110 thousand. And a diamond chipped medallion that read *'DTO'* being the center of it all. This was a real fucking ice show.

Slim says to Big O, "What does that 'DTO' stand for?" Pointing to the medallion.

Big O says, "Drug Trafficking Organization. It's my record label, DTO Entertainment. I changed it after I went to the joint and seen you. I got shirts, jackets, and jumpsuits. I trademarked the name. Shit's doin' good."

JB remarks, "He stay on that hot boy shit."

Big O, looking angrily at JB, replies. "What the fuck you mean? You're the one hangin' out with them hot chili pepper boys. If it were up to me, you wouldn't be at this meeting. And you know what? I'm gonna do this negotiating, because the word on the street is, you profited with the government back in '99 on that shotgun Crip case."

JB responds, "I don't know who said that shit to ya, but you got me all fucked up!"

Big O, grilling JB now, says. "No, I got you just right. Listen man, I'm done word wrestling with you. If something were to happen with my boy, Slim, know that you done messed with the best. So, bitch, you die like the rest!"

"So, O, "JB rebuffs. "You tryin' to threaten me or somethin'?"

"I don't make threats, bitch, that's a promise!"

Big O gets into JB's face, "Did I make myself clear now, snitch?"

Slim steps in between them. "Whoa, whoa, whoa! We didn't come here for this shit. We came here for a business meeting."

Just then, O's phone rings. O puts it on speaker and says, "Yo."

The caller says, "What's up? Where you at, G?"

"I'm taking care of some business. Is B with you?" O asks.

"Yes!" The man answers, "He right here. Bro, you not supposed to be rollin' without security."

"Ya'll just meet me up at Benihanas," and O hangs up.

JB, Slim, and O step into Benihanas restaurant. They walk up to the bar, have a few tequila shots, and order fried rice with chicken. They discuss business, Slim telling them he has packages for both of them.

"I didn't realize just how much product I had left over from that semi that came through a couple years back. I've been keeping it low key for a while, as to not attract attention to us. But, now that I think the heat is off, I figure I can ramp it up again. I got a buddy of mine back in Memphis helpin' out. I'm sorry I didn't let either of you know that I was working with the both of you before today's meeting. But I wanted to be careful, ya know?" Slim says.

Big O replied. "I understand, and I can cash you out right now, bro. That's the difference between me and this clown. All he want to do is get fronted."

JB scowls at Big O and says, Man, if you wanna get it on, we can go right now."

Big O scoffs, saying, "Don't threaten me with a good time."

Slim interrupts the exchange, "C'mon man. Players don't communicate like that. Let's get back to business."

Big O says, "Slim, please. This rat don't play the game. He gets played by it. The bitch that he is."

Slim gets up, leading Big O by the elbow, "Come outside, man. I got something for both of you."

JB gets up and follows Big O and Slim out the door. As they push through door, an Audi rolls up. The driver side window rolls down and the driver said,

"What up, Big O?"

Big O replies, "Just business, bro. But I have that punk ass JB over there."

The driver immediately pulls up to JB, and the driver says, "Yo punk! You got a problem with my man?"

JB says, "I ain't lookin for no trouble, but I ain't trying to duck none either."

The driver shifted to park, then jumped out of the car. Another man, named B, who was riding shotgun, also hopped out. They were both packing Glock 40s. Big O, stretching out his hands and arms, said,

"Whoa, whoa, whoa! Not here, not here! Put those things away!"

The men put their guns back into their waistbands and climbed back into the Audi, and waited on O. Slim, JB, and O walked back to their cars with the Audi following. O opened his passenger door, and grabbed a duffel bag. Slim opened his trunk, took out one of his duffel bags, and handed it to O as O was dropping his bag into Slim's trunk.

Slim asked, "So who are those guys?"

Big O replied, "Them my goons. Thirst-Ball's the driver and B is riding shotgun."

Slim said, "Them some motherfuckin' thunder cats."

"Ask JB, he know about one-nine." Big O continues.

JB says, "I ain't easily impressed."

Big O ignored JB and said to Slim, "that's half a ticket in the bag." That meant a half-million dollars.

"Thirst, let's roll, bro." Big O said.

"Hold up, bro." Slim replied, and gave JB his bag.

JB took it and asked, "What's the ticket?"

Slim replied, "Once you count what's in the bag, twenty-thousand a key."

JB popped the hatch on his truck, and put the bag in, then closed it. He then hopped into his truck.

"Hey JB!" Big O said, as he was approaching the truck, "I forgot to give you somethin'."

JB replies, "And what's that?"

Big O stops by the opened driver's side door and clocks JB right in the mouth, grabbing at his jaw in pain, shouts out,

"What the fuck? What the fuck was that for?"

O replied, "Remember, you invited me for a good time?" And he turns and walks back to his own vehicle. Slim, busting out laughing, says,

"Man, ya'll gets the fuck outta here before we get popped."

Thirst-Ball, who was chopped up, laughing himself, shouts out, "O, you one crazy motherfucker."

"G!" O shouts as he is getting into his car. "I ain't letting no one talk to me like I got no

panties on." He then looks to B, as JB was backing out, saying, "B, I got a hundred bricks for ya. They'll be at the house on Newton."

B throws a peace sign out his window to O, and the Audi pulls away. JB pulls up behind O, his window down, saying,

"This shit ain't over, nigga. It's on onsite!"

"Nigga," O responds, "You see me now. Get to it!"

Slim was already gone.

CHAPTER 8

Thanksgiving has rolled around. Slim was celebrating at his home with Big T, Delores, and Delores' family. Big O spent the time prior to promoting a show he was throwing at Myth Night Club in White Bear Lake that would be held later that night. The line-up included Rick Ross, Lil' Boosie, Young Jeezy, and Young Buck with Yo gotti headlining. Opening the show was Big O and King Knight.

Slim enjoyed Thanksgiving dinner with his family. Afterward, Slim slips out in his Escalade to pick up some cash from O and JB before the show started. He went to JB first, who was in Edina. Slim got there and JB gave him five-hundred grand. He said,

"I should be finished up in a couple more days."

Slim replied, "Okay, work smart not hard, bro. Just be careful."

"Dig it!" JB replied.

"You know," Slim said, "Big O is throwing a show up at Myth tonight. You gonna go?"

"If it weren't for Lil' Boosie," JB scoffs, "I wouldn't even consider it. But yeah, I'm goin'."

Slim says, "C'mon man, I thought you guys put that shit to the side?"

"Well, when you pulled outta Benihanas that night, we had exchanged some more words. If it weren't for havin' that pack on me, I'da popped his ass up!"

"Bro, you and Big O shouldn't be beefin' like that. You can't get money like that. You either beef or get money."

"Bro," JB replied. "It's Big O that started this tough man shit. He don't want me to get work from you. He wants me to go through him. And ever since he got home from the Feds, he been acting like Macho Man Randy Savage. He got that clique with Thirst-Ball. They be ridin' around the whole city, thinkin' they can't be touched. Slim, my motto is 'you gotta bring some ass to get some ass.' I'm gonna go to the show but, I'm gonna bring SSB with me."

Slim replied, "Man, I hope you niggas just keep gettin' money and avoid all that dumb shit. I'm gonna bounce outta here. I'll see you at the show, player."

JB says, "Alright, bro."

Slim got back into his SUV and took Gleason Road to Highway 62, known as the Crosstown Commons, west to 169 north. When Slim merged onto I-694 east to White Bear Lake, he phoned Big O. Slim told Big O he was on his way. O instructed him where to meet.

When Slim got to Myth, he pulled up to the side entrance, and rolled down his window. Big O came out carrying four duffel bags, singing

"Hey, bay-bay.... baby I got your money, don't ya worry!" Then said, "That's a full ticket. I'm done, bro. I bet JB's musty ass ain't even finished yet." He walked behind

Slim's Escalade, opened the back doors, and tossed the duffel bags next to the one JB gave Slim.

Slim said, "I gotta pick up my boy back at MSP. I'll see ya in two hours." Big O replies, "Cool, bro. I got you on the list to get in, as well as you son. I'm lookin' forward to finally meeting this dawg of yours. He sounds like a real ass nigga! Here's a couple of V.I.P. passes." He hands the passes to Slim.

"Thanks, bro." Slim said. He rolled up his window, pulled out of Myth, and jumped back onto I-694 going west. He sparked up some O.G. Granddaddy Kush while flyin' down the highway. He smoked one blunt as he entered onto I-35E south, and he smoked another one through St. Paul. He merged onto I-494 west, and then took the terminal 1 exit for the Minneapolis-St. Paul International airport. He spotted his boy waiting outside as he approached the loading/unloading area, and pulled right up to him. The man walked around to the back, opened the doors, and dropped his jaw when he saw the five duffel bags there. He tossed in his suitcase next to them. He closed the door, then went to the passenger side door, and got in.

"You one stupid motherfucka," Snake says as he closes the door and sniffed the air.

"You been rollin' around smoking Kush and picking my paranoid ass up? You know I don't like drivin' and smokin'. And what's in them bags? I know I'm helpin' your ass cuz' we're best buds, but I ain't stupid enough to ride around with bricks on me. If those are bricks, Slim, I'm hoppin' back out and catchin' the next flight outta winter wonderland here!"

"Don't worry, Snake. It's only one point five million," Slim replies.

"Oh, is that all? Shit, for a moment there, I thought you was back hustlin'. So not only are you driving under the influence, you're rollin' around with all them Benjamins like Floyd Mayweather Jr. That's giving probable cause to the Poe-Poe, bro."

Slim replies, "Shut the fuck up and hand me that lighter," as Slim pulled out of the terminal.

"I'll do it," Snake says. "I'll jump out the car right now, you gonna be that stupid. Last I checked, this state ain't no Colorado. They haven't legalized it yet. By the way, I ain't stayin' long. This place is as cold as Alaska."

When they pulled back onto the highway, Snake says, "Damn, Jeff Gordon, slow down! You doin' a hundred miles an hour! You gonna get your ass pulled over!"

Slim says, "Bro, since I got up here, I haven't had one cop bat an eye at me."

Snake replies, "See, you be thinkin' you're untouchable, but ya not. You think you above the law, Slim?"

Slim says, "I am a nigga. I'm getting money like a Boss. Since I been in Minnesota, I've stacked ten Mill."

"Good. That's real good, Slim. When the Feds throw your ass back in the joint, you can live like El Chapo. Maybe get a tunnel built under your cell like he did. Maybe have a nice Harley waitin' for ya in the tunnel."

"Snake, that's all you do is wish bad on someone. You want a piece of the pie, but when the heat's on in the kitchen, all you wanna do is cry."

"Slim, all kiddin' aside. I worry about ya bro. You got lucky when you left Memphis, and they couldn't find you. I don't want ya to get popped again, bro."

Slim made it back to his pad. As they were pulling in his driveway, Snake says,

"Holy fuck!" His jaw dropped. "Who you buy this house from? Adrian Peterson? Slim, you be doin' too much!"

They walked into the house, spots Delores. Snake says, "Hey Sis! How ya'll doin'?"

Big T jumps up from the couch, runs over to greet Snake and says, "Hey, Uncle Snake!

"What's happenin'?" He gives Snake a big hug.

Snake says, "Damn T, you ain't little no more! What you been feedin' my nephew, Sis? Steroids?"

Delores replies, "Your nephew has been hitting the weights like crazy!"

"Yeah, Uncle," Big T replies, "I'm captain of the football team now. Sh…. I mean, stuff's be crazy lately."

Slim says to Snake, "We need to hurry up or we'll be late for the concert. Our ride should be here in a minute."

Delores walked over and hugged Snake.

Snake says, "I gotta go freshen up. Don't wanna be late for Big O's debut."

Big T asks, "Dad, can I roll with?"

"Sure son, but hurry up, we ain't got much time.

"Can I get one of your chains, dad?"

"Sure thing, son, but get to it."

Slim and Snake go upstairs. Big T runs downstairs to his shower. Slim points out the upstairs bathroom to Snake, who hops into the shower. Slim goes to his bedroom to change. As all three men met on the main floor ten minutes later, Slim spotted their ride coming down the driveway. Delores walks by, also noticing the approaching vehicle, and says,

"Damn! You didn't invite me to this?"

"Sorry baby doll," Slim replies, "This is men's night out. I'll take ya to the Cincinnati Jazz Fest."

Delores hugged each of her boys, stopping on Slim last to give him some extra loving.

"You boys have a good time tonight," she says.

The men throw on their mink coats with their mink Gucci boots, and mink caps and step outside. They had so much jewelry on, you'd think they were the entourage for Jacob jewelry. Snake sees the H2 stretched Hummer, all black, parked in the semi-circular driveway.

He says, "Damn fellas, they gonna think we're Mr. Hollywood tonight."

"Uncle Snake," Big T says. "We is. Everything my dad do, he do big."

Slim says, "Fire the Kush up, Snake. We gettin' chauffeured tonight."

"'Bout time you do somethin' right, player." Snake responds, and sparks up a blunt.

Slim turned to Big T and says, "Sorry son, this ain't for you."

Big T replies, "That goes without sayin', Dad. I just wear silk, and drink milk, and lift weights and look great!"

Snake replies, "Boy, you sound like a lil' pimp or somethin'."

As they start rolling out of the driveway in the Hummer. Slim says to the driver, "bump some of that Rick Ross!"

The driver replies, "Of course, Mr. Carter," and they roll down the driveway, thumping to *'I'm a Boss!'*"

CHAPTER 9

As they roll down I-694, Slim places a call to Big O. When Big O answers, he says, "Can you get me a third pass? My son, Big T is rolling with us."

Big O replies, "Don't even worry about passes. King Knight and I are gonna be on in twenty minutes. How far out are ya?"

Slim replied, "We're about ten minutes out. Thanks, player."

"You got it, G. See ya in ten." Big O hangs up.

When they finally pull into the lot, the crowd immediately swarms the Hummer.

"Who's that?" One of the crowd member's shouts.

Another says, *"That's gotta be Young Jeezy!"*

"Girl," says a woman next to her. *"He already in the club. That's Rick Ross! Rick Ross!"*

"All the acts are already inside!" Shouts a man.

When the back door of the Hummer opened, flashbulbs went off like strobe lights.

One woman shouts out, *"OMG! Here! Take my panties!"*

Slim, Snake, and Big T stepped out onto the red carpet.

Snake says, "After the show, shawty! After the show!"

She replies, *"I'm gonna hold ya to that!"*

Big O and his entourage, wearing DTO shirts, approach them as more flashes go off. The light reflecting off of all the ice everyone in the group was wearing.King Knight, a tall black man with short cornrows and dreads with a mustache, says,

"Let's go make our presence known."

Thirst-Ball, who has a husky build and also sports cornrows and a mustache, escorts all of them into the club. They all approach the stage.

The crowd shouts out, *"DTO! DTO! DTO!"*

As the entourage climbs the stairs to the stage the crowd gets crumped, shouting out

"Big O! King Knight!"

Big O takes the mic and says, "We got a treat for ya'll tonight. If ya got any cousins, brothers, boyfriends, plugs, or your man locked up. Or they doin' fed time, my heart goes out to them. I've been there. All my nigga's on the stage tonight that representin' DTO, *'Drug Trafficking Organization Entertainment'*, can relate to you niggas. We got nothin' but love and respect for ya'll!"

Big O had a duffel bag with him. He opens it up, and then throws $100,000 into the crowd. The crowd goes bananas, grabbing after Benjamin's left and right.

"Be sure to throw that money on your homies books! Let them niggas know they ain't forgotten," Big O says. He and King Knight start their performance. King Knight starts first.

King Knight says, "We ain't hurtin' around here!"

Big O then says, "Repeat after me. If you ain't having no money problems, me and my nigga's, we got money...

money...money 'round here!" Big O then points his mic to the crowd, and the crowd shouts back,

"money...money...money 'round here!"

Big O and King Knight could hardly spit their bars out, because the crowd was going berzerk.

Big O raps , "We got the whole club going craaazzzy!"

King Knight then cuts in "DTO is the label that paaays me!"

After Big O and King Knight finish their twenty minute performance, Young Jeezy walks onto the stage. The crowd roars,

"We want O! We want Knight!"

As Big O and Knight step off stage to the V.I.P. Section.

Jeezy says into his mic, "God damn! Them boys rocked this joint! Give it up one more time for them niggas, Big O and King Knight, ya'll! DTO in the house!"

The crowd roars again, "Big O! King Knight!" Then, in staccato goes "D-T-O!", and then the crowd repeats.

"Big O! King Knight! D-T-O!"

Jeezy continues, "To all my motherfuckin' dope boys! You can do your thang, niggas! I just got one rule!" He sticks his mic out to the crowd. The crowd gets stupid and shouts,

"Don't get caught!"

After Jeezy finishes his performance, Lil' Boosie then joins Jeezy on stage. The crowd gets really rowdy.

"When I was facing my life sentence," Boosie started, "I would call home and my auntie would ask me, what's wrong? I'd say 'nothing', I just wanna come home." Lil' Boosie points his mic to the crowd.

The crowd cuts in, *"I'm comin' home! Pray for me!"*

After ten minutes of his performance, Lil' Boosie shouts out! "Big O! Big O! King Knight! Come back to the stage! Give us one more! Young Buck got a special announcement!"

Young Buck stepped onto the stage, and grabs the mic from Lil' Boosie, and says,

"When we were back in Yazoo at the federal joint. You said, you were gonna come home and blow up! You definitely came home and got to the money! Cut the check, I salute you, homie!" He turned to Big O and King Knight as he was approaching the stage, and saluted him.

Big O and King Knight stepped back onto the stage. Big O took the mic from Young Buck as King Knight grabbed another mic. Big O says,

"DTO E-N-T appreciate the motherfucking love you givin' tonight! I hustled hard in the streets, in the game. You got me plenty of fortune and fame, but at the end, I really felt the pain. I wonder if I'm through with the game."

King Knight throws the hook out. "Hustle…. Hustle…. Hustle…. Hard!"

The crowd repeats, *"Hustle… Hustle…. Hustle…. Hustle….. Hard!"*

After the encore, Big O says, "Minnesota, I love ya! Go out there and get your CD's, and you can follow us on Instagram!"

As Big O, Knight, and the rest of the entourage including Slim, Big T, and Snake walked off stage, they go to the V.I.P. Section. Instantly JB approaches with his crew, along with several others wearing shirts that say *"SSB'*. One of the security guards asks Big O,

"Are those gentlemen okay to go in with you?"

Big O screams, "I don't fuck with that pussy ass nigga!"

JB fires back, "I got your pussy tonight!" JB pushes through the bouncers and tries to jump Big O. Just then, all hell breaks loose as DTO and SSB members start rumbling. Big T jumps in and throws a punch at one of JB's boys. Thirst-Ball cold cocks one of the SSB members, knocking the guy out, out of nowhere, a tall black guy, sporting dreads, grabs a champagne bottle and cracks JB over the head with it, shattering on impact.

"You don't fuck with us, bitch!", the man shouts!

Big O shouts out, "Nice one, Lo!"

Security steps in to break up the brawl.

Snake says, "Man, get me the fuck away from all these high school kids!"

After things settle down, the owner of Myth Approaches Big O. He says,

"You can't do another show here. This shit's over!"

With that, the owner walks on stage, grabs a mic and says, "Sorry folks, show's over. Please immediately exit the building!" As security begins to escort people out, some shout out,

"*Boo!*"

"*What about Yo Gotti?*"

"*Rick Ross?*"

Big O steps outside and walks to his car. Big O approaches his car. As he does so, another vehicle drives up next to him. The passenger side window rolls down. A man inside says,

"Hey O! That was a nice show."

Big O replied, "Thanks man!"

JB pops his head out of the window and says, "How's this for a good time, bitch!"

POW *POW* *POW*

The rapport of the gun goes as JB shouts, "Big O! Three times in the chest!"

Big O is flung backwards, hitting his car. He clutches his chest as he slides down to the ground, falling over to his side. The car speeds off, its tires squealing away from the scene. The crowd outside the doors of the club immediately scattered when the shots rang out. Some gawking at the scene before them. Others also hit the ground. Thirst-Ball and King Knight, immediately run over to Big O. Knight shouting,

"He hit! He hit! My nigga been shot! Somebody call the ambulance!" Knight gets there, kneeling beside Big O, and holds O's head up. Thirst-Ball is at O's side.

"Damn, man!" Thirst-Ball says, "I told that nigga not to go anywhere without me!"

Police, who were running crowd control, immediately run over to them. Some houting!

"Did anyone see what happened? Any witnesses?"

An officer calls on his radio for an ambulance.

As Snake, Big T, and Slim run outside faster hearing the shot from inside the club doors. They see Thirst-Ball standing beside Big O who is lying on the ground. They were stopped by the police perimeter.

Snake says, "Gimme the fuck outta here. I'm not talkin' to no Homicide Detectives. This is the shit I be talkin' about, bro!"

An ambulance pulls up a couple minutes later. The EMTs do what they can to stabilize O, and load him into the ambulance. Knight climbs in with him, and the EMTs shut the doors.

Thirst-Ball says to Slim, Snake, and Big T,
"Ya'll can ride with me."
As they run to Thirst's Audi, Slim turns to Big T,
"You alright, son?"

Big T, doing his best to hold back his tears after seeing his idol all bloody says, "Yeah, I'm alright, dad."

They all climb into the A8, and follow the ambulance. Big O fighting for his life.

CHAPTER 10

After the ambulance leaves, the crowd begins to disperse. A few minutes later, a Detective and the Crime Scene Unit arrive. The Detective approaches the perimeter, flashes his badge to a guarding officer, named Marshals, and is waved through, ducking under the yellow tape. He asks,

"Who's in charge?"

"I am!" a female patrol officer shouts back.

The Detective approaches her, flashing his badge as he is shaking her hand, and introduces himself.

"I'm Detective Walt Sanders, BCA Homicide."

"I'm Sergeant Nicole Kempernich. White Bear Lake PD," the woman replies.

"What have we got?" He asks her.

She tells him the name of the victim, what had happened to him, then looks down to where he was standing and yells at the detective angrily,

"Hey! Watch where you're standing! You're about to contaminate my crime scene, standing that close to the blood!"

"Oh! Sorry," Sanders says and side steps a few more feet away. "Any witnesses? Do we know who did this?"

"We don't know who. I've got about five witnesses with about five-thousand different accounts of what happened. But, the only common item is that a car sped away. Good luck getting a description of the car, though. None of the people we talked to can corroborate that."

"Witnesses?" Sanders says, shaking his head. "As always, about as reliable as Minnesota weather."

"Yeah, changing every five minutes," Kempernich replies back. "We haven't talked to the bouncers yet, but from what we have gathered, the victim… Oh I forgot to mention, he was still alive when the ambulance took him to Regions Medical Center in St. Paul. Last I heard, he's in critical condition. Anyway, as I was saying, the victim might have been involved in a fight that occurred inside the club prior to the shooting."

"Hence why you mentioned talking to the bouncers?" Sanders said. "Get an APB out the moment you get a good description of either the car or the shooter."

"Will do. You go ahead, I'll let CSU take over here."

Sanders left the perimeter as two CSU techs came in. One takes photographs, and the other searches around. They collect some samples of the blood, collected two shell casings, and photograph tire track marks on the asphalt. Sanders flashes his badge to a bouncer at the door, and is waved through. As he enters, he hears shouting by the stage.

"I don't care if Don King himself was shot!"

Two men were by the stage. The one shouting was wearing a Fedora and a pimp suit. He continues,

"My client, Rick Ross, was suppose to get paid the rest of his money tonight! Since the big man himself is incapacitated," he uses finger quotes, "And since you're the one who shut the show down before my client got a chance to collect or even perform, I'm holding you," he jabs his finger into the other man's chest, "liable for the rest of my client's money!"

"Sir, I'm going to say it again," the other man replies. "I only rented the club space for tonight's event. The 'big man' as you call him was responsible for books and paying the talent. If you have any issues with payment, he needs to be the one you speak. I shut the show down because I didn't want a full scale riot in my club!"

"Well, he ain't here," Fedora man replied, "But you is. I ain't leaving until my client gets paid, so I'm dealing with you!" He then steps toe-to-toe to the other man, and gets in his face.

As an officer steps in to separate the two, Sanders shouts out "Gentleman!", and flashes his badge. "I'm Detective Sanders of the Minnesota Bureau of Criminal Apprehension. What seems to be the problem?"

"Oh good," Fedora man says. "Someone with authority. Can you tell this clown that my client has a contract with a gentleman who was supposedly 'shot' tonight?" He again uses finger quotes. "Since this man here," he points to the other man, "Was responsible for denying said payment to my client, Rick Ross, will you please exert some authority and make him cough up the rest of his money?"

"I'm sorry Sir, that's a matter for the Courts to decide," Sanders answered.

"Man, that's the same thing that officer said," Fedora man points to the patrolman who separated them. "My client's the victim here! A law gets violated and you police pick and choose what law you enforce." He shakes his head.

"Sir," Sanders replies, "Contracts fall under the jurisdiction of Civil Court. Not Law Enforcement. You sue the person whom you had the contract with. There's nothing more I can say or do on that account. Now, if your client was assaulted, physically I mean, I can help with that. Was he hit or did he witness any assault or other actual crime take place?"

"Um, no. Not to my knowledge," Fedora man says.

"Then step away, please, so I can speak with this other gentleman, in private." Sanders says.

man scoffs, "Fine!" He then stomps away.

"Thank you Detective." The other man says. "That man was getting on my nerves. I was about to have your officer remove him from the premises."

Sanders replies, "No problem. You mentioned a full scale riot. I take it that a fight did break out here?"

"Yeah," the other man said. "It happened in the V.I.P section. I'm the owner, Sal Koffman, and I had to shut the show down because of it."

"Can you describe what happened, Sal?"

Sal laid out the details of who threw the show and what he saw. None of the people who were DTO or SSB were left when the police came. For 30 minutes, Sanders talked to the other bouncers, bartenders, and waitresses. Then Sgt. Kempernich rushes in, spots Sanders, and hurries to him.

"We got a problem. A TV crew from channel four is here."

Sander's rolls his eyes. "Oh wonderful. Give them the usual blowback, and get in touch with your Public Relations Department. Once word gets out about a shooter on the loose, the Press is gonna hound us."

"You bet," Kempernich replies.

Just then her radio chirps, "Dispatch to forty-eight?"

"This is forty-eight, go." She replies.

"We got a nine-one-one on the line with info you may need. They wish to remain anonymous, however." The dispatcher says.

"Send it to my cell," Sanders tells Sgt. Kempernich.

"I'll put it on speaker so you can hear."

"Okay," Kempernich replies. Then into her radio, "forty-eight to dispatch, patch it through to the onsite BCA agent's phone, over."

"Roger that," the dispatcher replies.

A few seconds later, Sanders phone rings. He hits the speaker button. "This is Detective Sanders of the BCA, hello?"

The person on the other end, nervously says, "um. Hi. Are you the one in charge?"

"Yeah. Is this about the shooting tonight, at Myth?" Sander's replies.

"Yes. Listen, I don't want who shot that guy to come after me, so don't call me as a witness. I'm calling from a pay phone, so don't try to find me. I'll hang up now if I see a cop approach."

"No, no. That's fine. You can remain anonymous. What can you tell me?"

"Well," the caller continued. "Before the shooting, I saw this car drive up to the person who got shot. I saw him say something, but didn't hear what he said. Then I saw him get shot three times, and the car sped off."

"Did you see who shot this?" Sanders asked.

"No, the windows were tinted. Too dark to see inside."

"Can you describe the car? Do you know what make or model it was?"

"Yeah. I think it was a 2015 Chevy Impala. Midnight black, I believe."

Sanders smirks. "Did you get a look at the license plate?"

"Not fully, but I think some of it said grey... something."

"Can you spell that?" Sanders asks.

"G-R-E-Y."

Sanders does a fist pump. "That's fine. Are you sure you can't remember the rest of it?"

"No. I've said all I can say. I'm hanging up now." The call disconnects.

"Get an all points bulletin out immediately on that vehicle description. By the way, do you know who the SSB is?"

"Oh shit! They're involved?" Kempernich says.

"From what was said by Sal the owner, the bouncers, and all the other workers who witnessed the fight and there was one by the way, it sounds like it." Sanders replies.

"Dammit." Kempernich grunts. "Last fucking thing I need in my town is a damn gang war."

"It's the last thing we all need, Kempernich." Sanders replies. " I'll get the GTF on the horn, they get some good Intel."

"You better get the BCA Gang Task Force involved. I hate dealing with thugs."

Just then, Marshals rushes in. "We've got three newspaper reporters and two TV crews out there now wanting a statement," he says.

"Ugh," Kempernich sighs. "I hate dealing with media people, too."

"So do I," Sanders replies back. "We'll be out in a sec."

Kempernich's radio chirps again. "Dispatch to all units. Report of shots fired on the Frontage Road off I-694 to Rice Street."

"Dammit! Another one?" Kempernich sighs. "Marshals, get a couple of patrolmen and check that out."

"Yes, ma'am," and Marshals walks out the door.

"These shootings are getting out of hand," Kempernich says.

"Yeah, tell me about it," Sanders replies.

"Flip ya for dealing with the media?" she says.

"Can't. I gotta go to the hospital and see if this Big O, as they call him, is still alive and kicking."

"I suppose that's pretty important. But all the same, thanks for feeding me to the wolves." She says, giving him a sly smile. She then sticks her tongue out at him.

"Hey, that tongue better be registered." He says.

"Why's that, Detective?", she coyly asks him.

"Because if it isn't, I'll have to arrest you for illegally concealing a weapon," Sanders replies, returning her sly smile. Kempernich leans in closer to him and seductively says, "I might have to let you do that, officer." She then turns on her heels, and does a small strut before walking out the door.

After watching her derrière sway away from him, Sanders thinks to himself. Well, at least I don't have to worry about getting fired for sexual harassment." He then walks out after her.

CHAPTER 11

Back at Region's Medical Center in St. Paul. Big T, Slim, Snake, Thirst-Ball, King Knight, and B sat in the ER waiting room, holding vigil for Big O. Big T was watching the 10:00 pm news when he saw the lead story.

"Dad! The shooting is on TV!"

Slim goes to the television and turns up the volume. The picture cuts to a woman reporter outside.

"...Thanks, Amelia." She says. "A grizzly scene happened here tonight on what would have been a great debut for a local hip-hop artist and promoter. Thirty-eight year old Omar Sharif Beasley, commonly known as Big O, was shot tonight about an hour and a half ago here in the parking lot of Myth Night Club. He was promoting and debuting at a show here. Now, no word has been given yet on his condition, but we did learn that a fight may have broken out inside the club shortly before the shooting occurred."

The scene shifts to a black man with dreads, a goatee, and a neck tattoo. His voice cuts in.

"I was standing near the VIP section, and I heard some shouting..."

His voice lowers and the reporter's voice cuts in.

"Twenty-eight year old Reese Griffin saw a fight break out between what appeared to be rival gangs."

Reese's voice cuts back in.

"One side was wearin' DTO shirts, the other side SSB. And then fists started flyin'. One dude was cracked over the head with a champagne bottle."

"DTO," the reporter says, *"Stands for Drug Trafficking Organization Entertainment.*
Omar's record label and promoting company. Law Enforcement officials tell us they are not happy with the drug reference. SSB, we're told, stands for the South Side Boys."

The scene cuts back to the reporter,

"Now, Investigators are on the scene, but are being very tight lipped about what occurred. No arrests have been made nor have any suspects been named. However, a source tells us the SSB is a known gang that is rumored to deal in narcotics such as heroin and cocaine. This is a developing story, and we will keep you updated as more info becomes available. Back to you in the studio, Amelia."

As Slim turned the volume down, Snake walked over to him saying,

"Well, that's my cue to vamonos. The cat's outta the bag now. No more El Chapo shit for me. I'll take a cab back to the airport."

Slim replies, "Your stuff's still at my place, bro."

"Well, when they started making those lil' jeans and outfits, they didn't close down the clothing department. I ain't going back to your place, and have Homicide question my ass.

And by the way, when you ready to come get your money, don't bother comin'. I'll send it to ya. Your ass is hotter than a jalapeno pepper."

Just then, Sanders comes marching into the ER. He goes to the reception desk, flashes his badge, and asks for info about Omar.

"He's still in surgery, Detective. Been in there for an hour or so."

Snake sees this and whispers to Slim,

"Good thing we're in a hospital. I just came down with detective-itis. I'm gone, bro. You take care of yourself, Slim."

"You too, Snake." Slim tells him.

Snake says goodbye to Big T, whips out his phone, calls a cab, and walks out the door. Meanwhile, Sanders turns. He notices the tee shirts Thirst-Ball, King Knight, and B were wearing, and he approaches them. He introduces himself while flashing his badge, and asks,

"Are you gentlemen with Omar Beasley?"

Thirst-Ball crosses his arms, and stands with his feet wide apart. He replies,

"That's confidential information."

Sanders says, "Yeah? Well, we'll see how confidential it is when I contact the Gang Task Force and arrest you for obstruction of justice."

Thirst-Ball scoffs, "You better go do your homework, son. That state badge don't mean shit to me. I deal with the alphabet boys." Thirst-Ball then walks away.

Sanders turns to King Knight and B. "What about you two gentlemen?" Sanders referring to B and Knight, "You two have anything enlightening to add?"

King Knight and B look at each other for a moment, then turn their heads back to Sanders. In unison, they say, "I ain't see nothin', don't know nothin', ain't heard nothin'. And if I did, I won't tell you nothin'." And they too, walk away. Sanders says to himself, 'I can see why Kempernich hates dealing with thugs. What a bunch of dicks.'

He walks back to the reception desk, not giving any thought to Slim or Big T, and asks the receptionist if he can go back into the main ER area, and she lets him through informing him who his doctor is. He proceeds to the main ER desk, and finds his doctor.

She says, "It's touch and go at the moment, but from what the surgeon told me, he thinks Omar will pull through."

"Good!" He says, "Were any slugs removed from him. If so, how many?"

"Three were removed. There were no exit wounds."

Sanders pulls a plastic bag from his pocket marked 'Evidence', and holds it out to her.

"Can I have you or one of your medical techs place them in this evidence bag? I really need to get them to ballistics."

"Sure," she says.

"Make sure they use tweezers. I don't want them touched and have them contaminated."

"Detective," she replies, "This isn't my first GSW. I know how forensic works."

"Oh, sorry ma'am." He says.

Sanders sees Marshals walk by. "Hey, Marshals! What are you doing here?"

Marshals stops mid-stride and turns to Sanders. "Oh, hey Sanders." He continues, "Got a John Doe with gunshot wounds to the shoulder and thigh. He just came in, but he's unconscious. He had no ID on him, and they are prepping him for surgery."

"Sheesh, what a night, eh?" Sanders says. "I'll catch up with you later. I gotta get some slugs from a medical tech and get them back to the BCA crime lab. Take care, man."

"You too, Sanders." Marshals replies, as they both head their separate ways.

Back in the waiting room, Thirst-Ball goes to Slim and Big T. He says, "Ya'll better head home. With that dick roaming around, it's best you not seen near us."

Slim replies, "Good idea, Thirst-Ball. Have to call me to let me know he's okay."

Thirst says, "will do, player."

Big T says, "I hope O pulls through. He didn't deserve getting popped like that.

Thirst replies. "Kid, Big O is a tough motherfucka. He'll bounce back in no time. And we'll get the bitch that shot him."

"I wanna help get the clown," Big T says angrily.

Slim says, "Son, this is serious shit. You can get killed! Me and your mom don't want you hurt. Plus, you got a good thing going at school."

"Dad," Big T pleads. "I'm not a kid no more!"

Slim interrupts. "Son, we'll finish this later."

Slim turns to Thirst-ball. "You take care, G."

"You too, bro," Thirst says.

Slim and Big T fist-bump Thirst. Then father and son waited by the exit, as Slim called a cab.

After the call, Slim turns to his son. "I know you think you can be tugging' with Big O's crew, son. But, that is not the life me and your mom want for ya. Your football playin' is off the charts, T! You got a 3.8 average in school. Focus on that, son. Don't be messin' with this gangbang shit! You can do better than that."

"I'm sorry, dad," Big T replies. "It's just what happened to Big O is not right."

"I agree, son. But, let Thirst-Ball and the rest of Big O's crew handle it. They know what they doin'."

"Okay, dad." But, Big T thinks to himself: But, if anyone did you wrong, dad. I'd be the first one to pop off whoever fucked with you.

CHAPTER 12

Detective Sanders gets back to the BCA building with the bullets that were extracted from Omar. It's now been four hours since the shooting. Omar's Doctor told Sanders that Omar could not be questioned as he needed to stay sedated to recover from surgery.

He proceeds to the BCA Crime Lab, and tells the lead Tech, "These bullets were removed from the victim in the Myth Night Club shooting incident. Please get them processed immediately. We have a shooter on the loose, and I wanna catch this bastard." He hands the Tech the evidence bag.

"Okay," says the Tech. "We're just processing the casings now. Your boss put a rush on this. We normally don't process evidence this fast. But, I suppose a shooter still on the streets kinda makes it top priority."

"You bet your ass it does! With the rash of shootings in St. Paul and Minneapolis, the Governer want us to clamp down on this crap quick."

"Well," replies the Tech, "We did find fingerprints on the casings. So, if the prick is in the system, we'll find 'em."

"Excellent," Sanders says. "That would be the break we need. Outside of the anonymous tip and from what was witnessed in the club, very few people have been cooperating with me. The men in what I assume to be in the victim's crew, in particular, were real assholes to me."

Just then, a computer beeps.

The Tech says, "Speaking of prints, that sounds like a hit in the system. Lemme check. I was running a search on those prints when you walked in."

The Tech goes over to the computer, types in a few keystrokes, and the screen shows a match was found.

"Perfect," the Tech says, "the prints belong to an Earl Grey."

"Hold on, lemme ask one of my assistants to run a background on him, and have him picked up."

Sanders relays the information via a secure text message to his assistant. After his assistant replies back that he's on it, Sanders continues.

"Did you find out what caliber the bullets were from the casings or do you need to run those bullets through ballistics?"

"Yes, as a matter of fact, we did. They are forty-five Desert Eagles," the Tech replies.

"Holy fuck!" Sanders exclaims. "That bastard is lucky to be alive!"

A few seconds later, Sanders gets phone call back from his assistant. He says, "Earl Grey a.k.a. Baby Earl. DOB 08/16/76, height six feet zero inches, husky build, weight 236 lbs., residence: 2906 Clinton AV S, Minneapolis. Has conceal and carry permit. Register weapon is a .45 Desert Eagle."

Sanders replies back, "Get an APB out on his ass, and draft up a warrant for his arrest. Also, check his DMV records. I bet my measly salary that his car matches the description that a 911 tip left us. I'll have the Tech email you the information for the warrant."

"Will do, boss," his assistant says, and hangs up.

"I'll get that info to him right away, Dectective," the Tech says.

"God," Sanders says, "how stupid is this asshole? Using his own registered gun to shoot someone."

"Out of my thirty-seven years, I've never seen anything like this," the Tech replies.

"What a dumb ass."

"Lemme know if anything else comes up."

"You got it, Detective."

Sanders then walks out of the lab, with a confident stride.

After they sped off, and hit the highway, JB and Earl drove around for a half-hour. Then Earl comes to a realization and yells at JB.

"What the fuck, nigga? That gun is registered! My ass is gonna get popped, bro!"

JB replies, "Chill the fuck out, man. Nobody even saw us."

"Bro, the casings fell out of the car. Once those are recovered, this shit gonna hit the fan. You told me you were only gonna scare him. My father always told me, *'never pull a gun unless you gonna use it.'*" Baby Earl gets off the highway and pulls onto a side street.

"You shoulda had your own gun then, fool, and not gotten my ass jammed up. If them pigs come to my house, I can't go down like that, bro. I'm not takin' the rap for this shit!"

"What? Says JB. Don't be tellin' me you're gonna roll on me to my face, bro!"

And before Baby Earl knew it, JB brought the gun up to him. "I'll pop your ass with your own gun here and now!" JB then fires a round off, but misses, shattering the driver's side window.

"WHAT THE FUCK, BRO?!" Earl screams and opens his door while the car was still moving, but at a slower pace. He jumps out, trying his best to land on his feet and run. JB fires two more shots at him as Earl hits the ground running. One bullet hits Earl in the thigh, the other in the shoulder.

"Son of a bitch!" Earl shouts out. Earl falls down hitting the asphalt hard rolling end-over-end, his momentum carrying him.

"You ain't sayin' shit to no cops, clown!" JB yelled. He then notices the car was driverless and rolling toward a parked car on the side of the road. In a panic, JB drops the gun on the floor, and grabs the wheel, swerving just in time to miss the car.

Earl finally came to a stop in the middle of the road, flat on his back. JB slides into the driver's seat, shuts the door, and gets control of the car. He whips a U-turn about two blocks further down the road. With the tires squealing, he guns the engine.

Earl rolls over, and looks down the street. He sees his own car heading right for him! "Ha!" JB shouts out. "Shot by your own gun and now run down by your own car, bitch. I should rip your arm off and beat your punk ass while I'm at it, ya fuckin' rat!" JB barrels down the road.

"Oh shit!" Earl shouts out, and rolls back over to the side as his car goes whizzing by, just barely missing him.

Sirens blare in the distance. JB says, "Damn, I gotta get outta here." He speeds off down the road and back onto the highway.

Baby Earl, with great effort, pulls himself up over the curb into someone's yard. He passes out from the shock and blood loss. A person runs out of the house on the property to his side, as flashing lights become visible down the Frontage Road.

"Don't worry," the person tells Earl, "Help is on the way."

A patrol car stopped by to the two of them a few seconds later. Marshals got out of the car and ran over to them asking, "What's going on?"

CHAPTER 13

Back at Regions, Marshals sat in the cafeteria. It's been six hours since the shooting at Myth. He was waiting for his John Doe to recover from surgery, after repairing GSWs to his thigh and shoulder. The John Doe was now in the recovery ward. Marshals was eating a Bavarian-cream filled doughnut.

His radio chirps and info was aired out on his radio. "Dispatch to all units. APB is out for Early Grey aka Baby Earl. His car is a 2015 Chevrolet Impala, all-black, tinted windows. Licence plate George, Romeo, Echo, Yankee dash Romeo, Umbrella, Lima, Echo, Sam.

I repeat, 'Grey-Rules'. Suspect considered armed and extremely dangerous. Wanted for questioning in the Myth Night Club shooting incident. I say again, All Points Bulletin..."

Marshals flips open his notebook and writes down the info. Just then, two nurse walk in, and he hears one telling the other.

"Yeah, what an odd coincidence that we get two GSWs next to each other, and the surgeon says that if he didn't know any better, he would have said that the wounds were made by the same caliber bullet."

The other nurse says, "Yeah, the guy with the wounds to his shoulder and thigh woke up, saw the guy next to him with the chest wounds, and nearly threw a fit. He said he wanted to be released."

Marshals looks up at one of the nurses. He asks, "what? Is that guy the John Doe you're talking about?"

"Yeah," she says. "Except he's no longer a John Doe. He says his name is Earl Grey."

"Shit!" Marshals swears. He drops the doughnut on the table, and bolts out of the cafeteria.

Marshals races through the hospital to the recovery ward, blasts through the doors, and see Earl arguing with a doctor.

"I don't need to be here!" Earl says. He points to Big O, who was still unconscious. "I'm more at risk next to that guy then on the streets. Get me the fuck outta here!"

He then turns his head towards Marshals. Their eyes lock for two beats, then panic sets in on Earl. He tries to jump out of his bed, knocking down the doctor beside him. Ignoring the pain in his thigh, he bolts down the aisle around the nurses' desk.

"Freeze, dammit!" Marshals shouts out, whips out his Taser. He chases after Earl. "I'll tease your ass if you don't stop, Earl!"

"Fuck that!" Earl shouts out and grabs a metal tray off a desk, intending to use it as a shield. He turns his head back to see how Marshals is aiming at him, as Earl runs for an exit door out of recovery. But Earl doesn't notice the door flying open as a nurse is pushing a gurney through it. He is gut checked by it. "Oof," he grunts and falls smack onto the empty bed, stunned. The nurse pushing the gurney stops dead in her tracks, looking like a deer in headlights. Marshals catches up, putting his Taser away and whipping out his handcuffs at the same time.

"Earl Grey, you have the right to remain silent..." he says, as he is pulling Earl's hands behind his back and handcuffing them.

After finishing telling Earl his rights, he looks at the nurse who was pushing the gurney.

"The White Bear Lake PD and the people of Minnesota thank you, ma'am, for your assistance. That was good thinking on your part to stop him like that."

The nurse replies. "Well, oh, thanks officer, but I was just moving this gurney to recovery room six."

"All the same," Marshals says, "Thank you for the help." He then gets on the radio, "Forty-one to dispatch. I have the suspect Earl Grey in custody."

Twenty minutes later, Sanders comes plowing through the doors of the recovery ward, flashing his badge. Kempernich, who arrived five minutes before was standing outside of Earl's secured room with Marshals. She flags him down. He approaches them and says,

"Did I hear right? Omar and Earl were right next to each other here in recovery and we never knew about it?"

"Afraid so, Detective," Kempernich replies. "Fortunately, Earl came to first, and wanted to be nowhere near him. After Marshals slapped the cuffs on him, Earl said he would tell us everything, but only if he was put into a secured area, away from the victim. He said he didn't want another person trying to kill him."

"Another person trying to kill him?" Sanders replies confusingly. "What the hell is he talking about? All the evidence we have from the ballistics, to the tread marks that matches the type of tires his car would have, indicate that he's the one trying to kill people."

"I'm getting the feeling he might not have shot Omar, Detective," Marshals cuts in.

"When I got to the scene of that second shots fired call, out by Rice Street, his car nor is gun were nowhere to be found. He was also lying on the ground with gunshot wounds, scrapes, cuts, and bruises. We were waiting on questioning him about it until you got here."

"Where's Omar now?" Sanders asks.

"In another wing of the hospital," Kempernich answers. "His doctor said he should be coming to soon."

"Has Earl asked for a lawyer yet?" Sanders asks another question.

"He told me," Marshals said, "That if we don't charge him as an accessory, he wouldn't ask for one. He said he would fully cooperate."

"Then let's do it. Sanders says. "Marshals, stay out here to guard, please." Kempernich and Sanders then walk into Earl's room.

Sanders introduces himself, flashes his badge, and says, "Sounds like you had a rough night, Earl?"

"Yeah, you damn right I had a rough night! I'm tellin' you, I'm not the shooter. James Wilkens, goes by JB like James Brown, is the man you want," Earl said.

"And why is this 'JB' the one we want, and not you?" Sanders says.

"Because, first of all, that punk shot me with my own gun!" Earl explained. He then proceeded to tell them about what happened inside the club, how he loaned his gun to JB, how the shooting occurred, and the events that followed it." When Earl was finished, he asked, "So can you keep me protected? I don't want any of them DTO or SSB thugs coming in and cappin' me."

"Since it appears that an attempt on your life has already been made," Sanders says,

"Yes. Do you know where JB lives?"

"Nope, sorry man," Earl replies.

"Alright. We're gonna step out. You hang tight," Sanders says.

After Kempernich and Sanders step out and close the door, "Repeat the APB on Earl's car," Sanders tells Marshals. "We need that thing found pronto."

"I'm on it," Marshals says. He walks away to phone it in.

Sanders then turns to Kempernich. "I'm gonna go interview Omar. See if he has any info about this James Wilkens. Wanna tag along?"

"I told you, I hate dealing with bangers," she replies.

"I'll sign for your overtime," he says, giving her another sly smile.

"You already have to do that," she says. The she playfully punches him in the arm.

"Wow, first illegally concealing a weapon and now assaulting an officer. You really are racking up them violations tonight. What's next, extortion?"

"How about solicitation?" She says, using the same seductive tone she used earlier, and winks at him. Then she turns around and walks away. But then she turns her head back to him, and says. "I'll meet you at Omar's room. I need to freshin' up."

As Sanders watches her backside swing from side-to-side, he thinks to himself (yeah, definitely no sexual harassment here). He then goes to the nurse's station, asking where Omar's room is.

CHAPTER 14

JB was going through a lot of stressing, after ditching Baby Earl's car at an abandoned gas station. JB had one of the SSB's pick him up. They drove back to JB's condo in Burnsville. He peeked out of the car's window, paranoid as hell. After seeing the coast was clear, he hopped out and quickly got to his truck. It was a 2015 Ram 3500 Crew Cab Tradesman 4x4, with a 6.4 liter Hemi. As he started the truck, he thought to himself (I need to remain low key). Fortunately, he had tinted windows, so he wouldn't be noticed by either the police or members of the DTO crew. He jumped onto I-35W South, when his burner phone rang. He immediately knew who it was and asked himself. 'Should I answer it?' He didn't want to make the caller suspicious of anything, so he answered,

"What's up, bro?"

The caller replied, "Meet me somewhere up by Lake Street. Let's say at the Smokehouse. Can you be there in fifteen minutes?"

JB, trying his best not to sound nervous says, "sh...sh... sure, man." He passed the County Road 42 off ramp.

"Awesome, bro. See you then." The caller replied and hangs up.

"Shit!" JB said to himself. He passed the point where I-35E merged onto I-35W, becoming Interstate 35. He exited onto 160th Street, and doubled back the way he came. As he crossed over the Minnesota River, he thought to himself:

"I don't wanna clash with my boss!"

JB got to the meeting point fifteen minutes later. He didn't notice anyone. However, soon after his arrival, a 2015 Dodge Charger SXT pulled up in front of him with the driver's side window facing him. Two other vehicles that were following it pulled in behind JB. JB was nervous as hell. He grabbed his pistol, keeping it ready in case shit hit the fan.

The driver's side window of the Charger rolled down. JB rolled his window down, popped his head out, and asked,

"What's up? You called boss?"

Slim replied, "Yeah, I called. Get over here." He signaled with two fingers waving JB over.

JB rolled up his window, opened his door, and got out. He kept his pistol out of sight from the vehicle's behind him. He tucked the gun into the front of his waistband, and pulled his shirt over it. He then walked towards Slim's car. When JB got to the car, Slim noticed the bulge and said,

"JB, my first question is... Why?

"I told you that you couldn't get money while beefin'. Now, you got nigga's wanting to kill you over some dumb ass shit."

JB replied, "Who that in the Dodge Durango and Dart? Slim?"

Slim said, "Never mind that, for now. Let's talk business. You got more paper?"

"Yeah. I picked up some more before the concert. It's in the back of my truck. You still gonna fuck with me?" JB asks.

"It's gonna have to go cash and carry, man. Homicide's pokin' around about the shootin'. Never know if they gonna pick you up. What's done is done, bro. But that fight was in front of a crowd watchin'. They gonna tie the shooting to you, player. That being said, no disrespect, but I only cut with nigga's who think for themselves," said Slim.

"So what you sayin', bro?" JB asked.

"I don't need this heat towards my money. Now you know this shit gonna get hot as hell," Slim answered.

JB replied, "Lemme tell ya somethin'. When I shot that punk ass, I knew youd probably say, 'I don't wanna fuck with JB no more.' But my point is, he disrespected me for the last time. He punched me back at Benihanas, then he go talk crazy shit to me at the club. I ain't takin' that shit no more, Slim."

"Pride," Slim said, shaking his head. "You've got to let that shit go or you won't win, player. You will lose. See, where I come from, we don't get down like that. We just stop fuckin' with each other. This should have never come down to ya'll tryin' to kill each other. You know what I'm tryin' to say, JB?"

"Not really, Slim. I'm playin' for keeps out here. Anybody get in my way; I'm crushing' them."

Slim sighed, closed his eyes, pinched the bridge of his nose, and then shook his head for a few seconds. Then he waved the two vehicles blocking JB away. As they pulled back, Slim says, "Go get the money ya got."

JB walked back to his truck, got one duffel bag out, and threw it into Slim's back seat, shutting the door afterward. As JB walked away, Slim said,

"Sounds like you on some dummy pack shit. So, with that being said, I'm gonna let you do you, bro. I cannot afford getting caught up on some beefin' crap."

B stopped for a beat, cocked his head to the side, then turned back around facing Slim. Scrunching his forehead, he asked, "So whatcha sayin', Slim? Business is over between us?"

"If that's how you takin' it," Slim answered.

"Look here then. Slim get paid like Tyson, then up and straps," JB said.

"You done lost your marbles," Slim replied.

JB said, "Pull off bro, before you make the news."

"Bro, I don't want you to do this and regret it later."

"Slim, pull the fuck off. This my last time asking you, okay?"

"When you give me the rest of my motherfuckin' money." Slim replies.

"Pull the fuck off. Ya'll gonna quit playing with JB like he's a hoe or somethin'. For real,
bro! Lemme make one word clear to you, Slim. Make sure you save enough for a pretty casket!"

Then, without warning, JB pulls his gun and shot out Slim's rear passenger window. He then dove back into his truck, backed out, squealing his wheels and took off. Slim, who had ducked behind his door when the shots rang out, popped his head back up to see JB's truck back out into Lake Street. Slim thought to himself: 'I ain't havin' this shit from that whore. His ass is out.'

Slim pulled out of the parking lot and headed to meet B over on the North Side, getting some more straps from his guys. He couldn't believe the shit JB pulled. He would let it be known that JB was a mark if he was out for blood.

CHAPTER 15

After weeks in the hospital, Big O has recovered from his injuries. JB is now a wanted man. Not only is the hunt on for JB by Big O, but the police also are aware he is the shooter, from the information given to them by Baby Earl. Slim stayed away from the hospital so as not to bring attention to himself in case the Homicide Detectives were still there. Slim knew Big O wouldn't give no detective info about the shooting. Big O doesn't ride like that. He ain't no snitch. He's a nigga who handles his own problems, his own way. Slim was angered at JB for the shit he pulled, but thinks to himself, let karma take care of his ass.

Slim decides it's safe to call Big O. He had heard he was back in the studio again. Some things never change.

"Big O! Slim says.

"What's poppin Slim?" answers Big O.

"Ain't shit, bro," Slim replies.

"That nigga ain't up to been who he say he is, bro! I told you my nigga, where you at, Downtown at the studio?" Big O states.

"Well, I'm gone home. Holla at you, okay?" Slim replies.

"Come down, bro, I'm working on this new song!" Big O replies.

"My manager, Zack Beats, are all down here smoking on some cookie," Big O states.

"" Yeah," replies Slim, "on my way. By the way, I'm on Portland, my GPS say six minutes away from you!"

"Zack, say, do it over. Ride the beat, bro!" Big O says.

"Big O, say turn me up a little in the head phones!" Slim requests.

'DTO Entertainment.'

"We are up next," states Big O.

Big O rap:

'I heard they want to ride on us, bitch

Nigga bring it on 'cuz I strap with the

Mac on my seat

I'm at the club everywhere

The doctor said I never walk again

Talk again

I get nit with AK and still see another day

O, you must be blessed'

"Damn," Slim said, "That shit goes hard as hell, bro. Niggas gon be bumping that shit this summer."

"Yeah bro, that nigga don't know what he done. He created a monster," Big O replies.

"You fucking with the club tonight?" Slim asks.

"Yeah, I'm hunting and trying to find that nigga JB hoe ass."

"Yeah my nigga," Slim replies. "Them joints I gave dude? His punk ass pulls a move on me and pulls his strap on Lake Street and shot out my window!"

Big O replies, "I told you dude! He's one fucked up person. I can see these bogus ass niggas from a mile away. A Homicide Detective comes and questions me when I was in the hospital. And again when I was outta the hospital. Says his name is Sanders, and started asking me about the shooting. I tells dude, I don't know who hit me! This Detective stated that he had information from a witness that JB might have been the shooter. That motherfucker was hounding me alllll night bro! Finally, I told him it aint none of his business. I aint got nothing more to say. He can talk to my fuckin lawyer. You know I ain't bout that!"

"Yeah I hear ya, bro," says Slim. "They don't know when to quit."

Later that night, Slim and Big O goes to the strip bar called Auggies. The club was jumping and for real, all the girls were everywhere and with them! Big O had thrown twenty thousand in the club. Everybody was happy that he recovered from the gunshot wounds! They had bottles coming back to back. B, Thirst-Ball, and Little Low were there too.

"All my niggas are in the club," O says to himself.

"Man, we goin' to have to take those poles out the dip soon." O says. It was getting near closing time, so they all decide they want to go to the parking lot.

"I know the MPD Police Department is right there, but I've taken enough chances. I'm not counting on them suckers!" Big O remarks. Word was out that Big O was down at the club, so a lot of Big O's niggas had come down to see him. Before leaving, O's nigga Baby C came in the club. Also another bro, Bro papa. They were all kicking it, havin' a good time. There were hoes everywhere. Then Big O sees this punk ass nigga from Detroit he didn't like.

"Is that nigga, Black? O says.

"Yeah!" says several of the guys. O goes right over to Black, and starts stomping the shit out of him.

Big O says, "Yeah, I finally found your punk ass! You was running!" Thirst snatches the nigga's chain off, and B takes the punks watch. Then they both kick him in the ass! Big O tells him to keep his name out of his mouth. Then head-butts him and hits him in the face with a Moët bottle. The bouncers intervened and they were all kicked out of the club. Black didn't come out of the club.

As they start walking to their cars, one of Big O's entourage spots someone familiar.

He says, "Bro, guess who I see over there? JB?"

"Quit lying!" They all say together. "You lying?"

"Nope. He's gettin' in that black Charger." he continued.

"Get them poles out, okay?" Big O says. They waited for JB. He was exiting out of the parking lot from Auggies. He put his turn signal on to turn left. He was heading towards the highway, then onto I-94 West. He exits onto Broadway AV. They were staying close on his ass. JB didn't notice their car following him. Before you know it. JB turn onto Penn AV. Before they could get any closer. Slim and JB were shooting! POW! POW! POW! POW! POW! POW!

"Damn, they blowing up!" Big O says.

JB was moving fast as hell. Slim and JB were still shooting at each other. JB lost them when he jumped out of his car. He ran through a yard on James Ave, and straight to his Auntie's house. When his auntie saw JB, she said "Why are you breathing so fuckin' hard?"

"They just ride to smoke my ass!" JB hollered.

"Who?" JB's Aunt replied.

"Big O and Slim," JB continued, "It's on now!" JB called Slim and said, "I'm killing your whole family! It seems to me like Big O ain't learned his lesson? Guess what niggas, it's

on!" Slim said real smooth, "That's why we on! You mess with

the best you die like the rest!" click!

CHAPTER 16

Slim was at home talking to his wife. He asked her how was she liking the new job? She replied, "it's more money since I moved up here to be a RN (Registered Nurse). Slim what are you going to do for a living?"

"I just really want to pursue the music business with my guy Big O! We was in the slammer together. He has some talent when it comes to spitting on that mic," Slim replies.

Big T says, "yes, he does! He's got swag also."

"The reason I stay on with you Slim is because you made it. You got everything you ever wanted," Delores states.

"Baby I was never messing around in the game to claim the fame. I was trying to provide a decent living for our family. So, are we going to church today? It's family day!" Slim replies.

'Yes," says Delores. "Let's go and get dressed. The lord is trying to tell you something Slim. Get right with him."

"So are you still hustling Slim?" asks Delores.

"Naw," Slim replies, "just a few cats owe me some paper."

"Slim," says Delores "I couldn't sleep comfortably in this house last night. The lord revealed to me that you got locked up. He said you were selling drugs and someone is trying to set you up, baby." Delores started crying, "I don't want this for our family."

They were going to a church called 'Church for God and Christ'.

The choir was singing 'My Mother Prayed for Me'
and it had me on Her mind
Took the time to pray for me
I'm so glad she prayed.

The church was clapping. Preacher got up and said to touch your neighbor and tell them you are glad they prayed for you! He spoke this and said God wants a young man to change over his life and come to Christ.

As Pastor Troy was speaking he was looking right at Slim. Slim said, "Damn, this Pastor is talking right to me." It's like he is hitting home, because the things he was saying had Slim teary eye.

Pastor asked, "is there anyone who lived in the streets like him?"

He said, "it was a way I lived before I came to Christ. I was in prison for dope selling. I got to prison and made my decision a few weeks later, in my bed. I got down on my knees and asked the Lord to come into my life. I was still selling drugs in prison. I flushed all my drugs down the toilet."

"Amen," said the congregation.

Delores was clapping for her family, and praying that Slim get this message before it's too late.

Pastor Troy said, "you have to avoid those old partners and those old trap houses."

Everybody started laughing.

Slim shouted, "preach Pastor!"

He said, "dope boys, I know you in the church today. I want to tell you, in the way you live, pleases the Lord. He makes even your enemies live at peace with you."

Only thing Slim could think about, was him and JB getting into it.

Pastor said, "a foolish person finds pleasure in doing evil things. But, a man who has understanding, takes delight in wisdom."

Slim says to himself, he has to live for the Lord.

"Give your life to Christ, before it's too late," Pastor said, "if anyone who takes a crooked path will get caught. Join the Lord and take up your Cross!"

Six guys walked up to the altar and gave their life to Christ. After that, Slim walked up and said, "thank you Pastor for introducing my life to Christ."

Pastor said, "you know it's not a game. Be easy, but you have to stay around Positive brothers. We welcome you all to God and Christ."

Delores asks Slim, "how do you feel about the change?"

"I'm feeling good about the decisions I've made," states Slim.

They all go out to Ms. Ann's Soul food and have some Fried Chicken, Greens, Candy Yams, Mac & Cheese, and pop.

Big T said, "I'm proud for you dad. This is the right way papa."

"Yeah son, I'm tired of watching behind my back. The Lord is calling me to do something different. I gave the devil all my life by being a dope boy," says Slim.

So they start heading back to the house. Slim is driving up to the house and he felt good. Delores was very happy he was making that change, also.

Slim states to his wife and son, "I got to go and holla at Big O for a few, and ask him if he wants to start a legit Company, promoting concerts."

"Okay baby," says Delores, and she kisses Slim and states she will be waiting on him to get back.

Slim's phone rings, "What up O?"

"You good, bro?" Big O replies.

"Just got out of church, and I'm feeling real good, bro. I joined, that's what's up, bro. We all need the Lord. I was thinking about us doing some concerts," says Slim.

"I do some Gospel ones," O said.

"I'm with it, bro! Okay," declares Slim. JB is beeping in on the line.

"What's good?" says Slim.

"You still on that, Slim? "asks JB

"Naw, bro, I gave my life to the Lord. I'm trying to start anew," states Slim.

"You holla at me in a minute. In 2 hours my guy and I want to pay your cheese, okay?" says JB.

JBs phone beeps, "hold on bro, let me answer the jack."

"Teddy, you good breasts JB.

"Yeah, I need five of those seat tickets to the game (which means 5 kilos of coke)," says Teddy.

"Where you at then? "asks JB

"Come on to 29th and Portland, okay?" Teddy requests.

JB drives over to the apartment buildings. Agents spot JB and they set the team up. An agent states, "man, Mr. JB, the big baller, out here pushing this poison like crazy, huh? Before JB could make out the car, a police car pulls in behind him. They didn't seem like they were after him.

So, JB calls Teddy, "Where you at?"

"I'm in Apartment 206," states Teddy.

JB says, "okay."

JB grabs the bag. Right then, the agents jump out of their cars and yelled, "Put your fucking hands up! What do you have in that fucking bag?"

The Agents grab the bag from JB and throw the bag containing coke on the hood of his car.

"Look at what we got here," states an Agent. The Agents start slapping each other's hands. They handcuff JB and take him to a Federal Building in Brooklyn Park.

The Agents say to JB, "We know all about your shooting, but we are not here for that. We want to know about Cedric Carter a.k.a Slim."

"No problem, I can give you all ya'll want," says JB. "Do you think Slim will mess with me?"

"Yes, because we know ya'll been beefing," the Agent continues. "Also, we know you still owe Slim some change, and you just hung up on him, correct?"

"Yes Sir," says JB.

"Big O isn't going to do business with you because you shot him, correct?" the Agent asks. Look here, the US Attorney knows you are here and knows you will try to cooperate to save your ass right now. You are looking at life; you are done unless you give us something."

So, JB places a call to Slim.

Slim's phone rings. "Hello?"

"Bro, I got your paper. Where can we meet? "asks JB.

"Have you ever been out here by Savage, Minnesota? "says Slim.

"Yes, okay I'm on my way," states JB.

Federal Agents place a mic on JB just before leaving to meet with Slim. The Agents are having trouble hearing the exchange between JB and Slim. So, the Agents turn the mic up. Agents test out the mic, "I can hear you."

JB says, "Okay."

Then they ask JB, "JB you hear me now?"

"Yes." JB says.

The Agents hear JB say to Slim, "I got the money, but I only got enough for fifty, okay?"

Slim replies, "Okay."

The Agents put the money in JB's truck.

Slim arrives at his destination to meet up with JB. As he is pulling up in a white Caravan. Slim begins to feel uneasy. Something doesn't feel right Slim says to himself. JB's phone starts ringing, it's from Slim.

"Where you at, bro? Slim says. "Don't want to be out here dirty."

"Got you, bro." JB replies.

Slim could feel something ain't right. He starts to pull off and notices a white Pontiac tailing him. Then out of nowhere, Agents tell the Trooper to stop Slim's vehicle. The Trooper immediately pulls Slim over before he could get away.

"License and your insurance, please?" The State Trooper says. Slim complies.

"With that, you mind us searching your car?" The Trooper asks.

Slim said, "NO!"

The Agents had arrived on the scene to assist the Troopers. Although Slim did not give him permission for a search, the Agents and the Troopers still conducted a search of Slim's vehicle. They didn't find anything, so they called in a K9. The K9 circled Slim's vehicle, and sat down by the trunk. So, the Agents searched Slim's trunk again. This time, there were 50 keys of coke tucked under a panel.

Slim was immediately arrested by the Agents and taken straight to Anoka County Jail.

Later, Agents learned where Slim lived and went to his home. Agents immediately execute a search of Slim's home without a warrant. They kick in his door with his family there, and begin tearing it apart. As they were leaving the house in shambles, one of the Agents confirms to the others, "No Drugs here boys!"

Delores was beside herself with anger and says, "Your dad said he stopped this shit!"

Slim was placed on a D.E.A. hold. He couldn't talk on the phone and it was lashing at him.

"It's bad for Slim," says Big T. "They took my dad away from me!"

Big T begins to cry. He couldn't handle what was happening and sent to his room to sleep. As he laid there in bed, he realized he was the man of the house now. Big T cried himself to sleep that night.

CHAPTER 17

Delores sat at home on her leather recliner chair, crying as her cordless phone rings. An automated message played when she answered. "You have a collect call from…," then Slim's voice cuts in, "Cedric Carter…" The automated message continues, "an inmate at Anoka county Jail, to accept this call, press five, to refuse this call, hang up now. To block this call and all future calls, press nine."

Delores presses five. After hearing that the call could be listened in on and recorded. Slim comes on the line.

"Hey, baby," he says.

"Hey, baby? Are you fuckin' serious? "she screams into the phone. "These fuckin' Federal Agents come in and kick our door down without no warning," Delores starts crying again. "They throw my Baby T to the floor like he was some thug, but he ain't done no wrong! You told me you were done with this hit, Slim. You promised me you were done! Why, Slim, Why? Now these Agents are asking me questions I don't know the answers too."

"Listen, baby," Slim says. "I need you to put a thousand dollars on my books. Call this Attorney named Caroline Durham. They says she a good Attorney in the State of Minnesota. I need you to give her a Retainer fee of $30,000., 'cuz I got court in the mornin'."

Delores says, "Are you done with this crap or not Slim? Is this over? I'll do it only if you are done, Slim."

Slim replies, "I'm finished baby. Tell my son I love him. I love you, baby doll."

Delores says, "I love you too, Hun."

They both hang up.

Slim returned from court, and fired his Public Defender after he was detained. He knew it was going to be a long fight after he was taken back to Anoka. When he got back to his cell after he heard the charges against him, he thought '*Man! This shit don't sound right. I've been set the fuck up!*'

The Corrections Officer came to Slim's cell and popped his door open,

"You have a visitor."

Slim says, "I'm not going. I'm not talking to no more damn Feds!"

The CO replies, "No, this is your Attorney."

Slim is then escorted to the visiting area. There was his Attorney, Caroline Durham, sitting there.

She says, "May I help you with this web you've created?"

"Yes. Are you a fighter?" Slim replies.

"Yes." replies Ms. Durham.

Slim says to her, "You know this is my life we are gambling with?"

"Okay, I do have the discovery and I do have the reports from the stop. This stop was illegal." Ms. Durham continues. "They never had the right to search your home without no warrant. There is a lot of doubt that can be raised in this case. I'm going to suppress the stop and the search. Mr. Carter how does that sound?"

"You're the lawyer and that's what I'm paying you for," responds Slim.

She tells Slim after this is over you will be a lawyer. "Here's your discovery and be careful because a lot prisoners jump cases in here. Do you want me to keep it for you?"

"No. I can handle it. No one's gon' jump on my case," Slim replies.

Before Caroline left, she turned to Mr. Carter and reminded him, "Please don't discuss your case with anyone, please."

Slim nods in agreement, and then is led back to his cell by the deputy. Caroline didn't know that Slim was already smart with the law. Not many knew that Slim had studied to become a paralegal during his last bid and she didn't know that he would challenge her to go to trial and fight for his freedom.

While in his cell, Slim replayed the night he was arrested over and over again. Going over every detail he could remember he suddenly realized what had went down that night. *'Damn! I should have listened to O! Goddamn, JB!'* He said to himself as he realized that JB had set him up that night. He continued to himself, *'That's how you want to play me? I'm going to spend every dime I have to get back my freedom.'*

On 8/17/2015, I, Special Agent Larry Scott, completed an application for search warrant and supporting affidavit which was presented to and signed by the Honorable Judge Michael Brown. This search warrant was issued to search a residence belonging to Cedric Carter, located at Prior Lake, 13942 Franklin Trail. Also, included in the warrant were Delores Carter and son Tyrell Carter. When searching the home there were no control substance in his home. Special Agent set up surveillance on the residence. Observed an all-black S550 Mercedes Benz traveling toward our direction. The team stayed in the back of him to watch him travel to the CRI to bring control substance to the meeting location.

After reading this it didn't take Madlock to figure out why Slim was sitting in Anoka County on his bed reading this. Slim shouted angrily, "MOTHERFUCKER! I shouldn't never ever fucked with this rat ass bitch!" He then closed his eyes and said "God please, give me favor and no weapon perform against me, shall profit! I can do all things through Christ that strengthen me. Let's fight Government." Then he closed his eyes and went sound to sleep.

Caroline walks up and Slim is in the visit room waiting on her.

"Hello, what you got for me?" Caroline says as she approaches Slim.

He says, "Look here, often times many cases are started with misinformation, and misdirection. Which all comes from confidential informants. Some are smart and savvy, but for the most part, all are looking for something in return. CI/C/CSI/CC/SOI. I studied all these as a defendant, I know the game. I see and I 'm smart to know that the Feds don't play fair what's so ever." Observing her reaction to his surprising knowledge of the law, he continues, "Caroline, Police investigation must be carefully scrutinized. In our system of justice, it is defense Attorneys that force the law to play by the rules. That's what I need you to do, blaze them on that stand. For the most part, Ms. Durham, snitches are either in a situation trying to help themselves out of doing jail time by providing substantial assistance. Just for the record, I know who the snitch is, he a.k.a JB, James Wilkensen and he got busted and he is trying to turn state's evidence and put his suffering on me."

"Well, what a friend. You are very smart," said Ms. Durham. "I know we don't need the government to try and cover the name. Have a nice day."

On the night of graduation, Big T attended the Senior Lock-in party. It was an all-night affair at the High School. It included dancing, games, contests, and even a magician and hypnotist. He was there, with his girlfriend, Brenda Perez. They found a dark an isolated stairwell and made love to one another.

Afterward, she had to run to the bathroom. She got back, she was wiping her face dry. Big T asked her, "What happened?"

She replied, "I got sick again. I don't know what's been going on, but this is the fourth time this week this has happen."

Big T said, "You want to go to the doctor?"

"No," she replied. "I'll be alright."

"When I go see my dad in jail tomorrow, would you like to meet him? Mom listed you as family."

"Sure, that's so cool your mom did that."

"Well, wait until you meet my dad. He Black as fuck."

After the all-nighter where they watched other classmates get hypnotized and do funny things like act like a chicken, Big T and Brenda drove back to his house.

Delores greets them as they enter the house, "How's my baby doin'? Ya'll want some pancakes and eggs for breakfast?"

"Nah, mom," Big T says, "Today is visiting day for dad. You wanna come up there with us? I'm havin' him meet Brenda, gettin' his approval."

Delores says, "She's got my approval, so she don't need his. Ya'll go on ahead. I'm sure he'll like her, too."

They spoke for a few more minutes, and then Big T and Brenda took the truck out. They drive up towards the jail, stopping at a Wendy's.

"Holy fuck," Big T says.

Brenda says, "What is it, Hun?"

Big T says, "That's the fuckin' snitch that turned my daddy in and shot Big O back in November."

Brenda says, "Oh my god!"

Big T pulls up and rolls his window down, and shouts to JB, "Hey punk! You're a piece o' shit rat."

JB relies, "Hey man, don't get that pretty truck shot up."

"You're the bitch that should be worried about getting shot up. You ratted on my dad and shot at Big O. In my book, JB, you're always gonna minus the bars, and When your son grows up. He's gonna always know what the fuck you don, and he not gonna be proud."

And out of nowhere, JB shoots at the truck.

"Get down, Brenda!" Big T shouts, "This motherfucker blow it!"

They speed out of the parking lot, heading towards the jail to visit Slim. After they got to the jail, they had to leave their cell phones in the car as they weren't allowed inside the jail. They were searched, and finally let in with the other people visiting. They saw Slim behind a glass wall with a phone receiver on each side of the wall. Slim and Big T picked their phones up at the same time.

Slim spoke first, "Hey, son. I'm so glad you came to see me. Where's mom?"

Big T replied, "I'm glad to see you, too. Mom said she'll come on her own. She's still pretty upset."

Slim said, "She'll get over it. Now, who's this that you brought with?"

Big T says, "This is my girlfriend, Brenda. Would you like to talk to her?"

"Sure," Slim replied.

Big T handed Brenda the phone. She says, "Nice to meet you finally Mr. Carter. I'm Brenda Perez."

Slim with a curious look says, "Nice to meet you too Brenda. It's weird though. You look kinda familiar, like I've seen you somewhere before. I happen to also know a Perez. He's down in Mexico. His name is Jose and he has a brother too, named Daniel."

She replied, "That's funny. They are my uncles."

Slim replied, "Holy fuck, what a small world."

TO BE CONTINUED